G. W. HEWLETT

The
FRIENDLY INVASION

The
FRIENDLY INVASION

Roger A. Freeman

Published by
East Anglia Tourist Board in conjunction with
Terence Dalton Limited

Text photoset in 11/12 pt Souvenir by
Dalton Origination

Printed and bound in Great Britain at
The Lavenham Press Limited, Lavenham, Suffolk

ISBN 0 86138 103 3

Contents

Acknowledgements and Introduction   ···   ···   ···   vi

1   Two Nations   ···   ···   ···   ···   ···   ···   1

2   The Yanks are Coming...   ···   ···   ···   ···   4

3   Them and Us   ···   ···   ···   ···   ···   ···   9

4   The Air War   ···   ···   ···   ···   ···   ···   17

5   Making Friends ...   ···   ···   ···   ···   ···   31

6   Inn-house Entertainment   ···   ···   ···   ···   41

7   Kinda Different ...   ···   ···   ···   ···   ···   45

8   Mind the Language   ···   ···   ···   ···   ···   55

9   Fellows They Brought With 'Em   ···   ···   ···   58

10   Overpaid?   ···   ···   ···   ···   ···   ···   61

11   Oversexed?   ···   ···   ···   ···   ···   ···   65

12   Over Here and Back There   ···   ···   ···   ···   77

Glossary   ···   ···   ···   ···   ···   ···   ···   84

Index   ···   ···   ···   ···   ···   ···   ···   ···   86

Acknowledgements

THE AUTHOR is indebted to the following persons for providing the anecdotes used in this book:- Roger Armstrong, Henry Bamman, William Barnett, Walter Bergstrom, Ivan Brown, Jack Bryant, Robert Cayer, Bud Chamberlain, Daphne Chute, Forrest Clark, Robert Coffin, George Collar, Iris Falcone, Kay Fielding, Daniel Freitas, Charles Harkins, Calvin Hill, Warren Hill, John Howland, Albert Jones, Tony Kerrison, Robert Kerr, Saul Kupferman, Edward Laube, Elinor Lilley, Nelson Matthews, Newton McLaughton, Tom Morrow, Jack Neasham, Tom Parry, John Ramsey, Wilbur Richardson, Nancy Ruska, Stanley Sajdak, Rose Searah, Leon Senk, Irving Shapiro, Curtis Smart, Helen Smith, Marion Smith, Harley Stroven, William Sullivan, Arthur Swanson, Cecilia Trip, Jordan Utal, Hathy Veynar, H. Ben Walsh, Roy Winn, Stanley White and Al Zimmerman. Material and assistance was also provided by Quenton Bland, William R. Cameron, Alan Crouchman, Arnold Delmonico, Vic and Maureen Maslen, Connie and Gordon Richards, Geoff Ward, Duane Reed (Air Force Academy Library) and Robert Sand. On the production side Ian Mactaggart, George Pennick, Bruce Robertson and Jean Freeman were involved. To all I offer my sincere thanks.

Introduction

THE FOUNDERS of what is now the United States of America were mainly British colonists, so that much in this great republic is derived from an initial British influence. English became the official language and many institutions were modelled on those of the old country. However, two centuries of separate development created differences largely unappreciated by the two populations until the interchanges of more recent times. When a vast number of United States military personnel came to the United Kingdom during the Second World War differences were highlighted during the forging of the common bond to achieve victory.

In many areas the impact of this friendly invasion was considerable, particularly in villages where United States servicemen outnumbered the local population. From the actions of some, the British tended to view the average GI as being brash and a womaniser, while the American experience was that the natives were old fashioned and reserved. These generalisations soon proved to be exaggerated once friendships were established, leading to the realisation that exceptions were not the rule.

In eastern and southern England the United States established – in terms of men and machines – two of the largest air forces in history. The bloody air battles launched from bases in the English countryside brought appreciation of these young Americans by the indigenous population that transcended any clash of cultures and customs. Indeed, the bond of goodwill established then has endured with undiminished strength for the lifetime of many participants. Moreover, Britain and America are now deemed inseparable allies in the international sphere. This book sets out to record and examine situations that arose, using, where possible, the words of those involved illustrated by contemporary photographs.

Roger A. Freeman   Dedham, England   January 1992

1 TWO NATIONS

NOW, IN the late twentieth century, an encounter with a native of a far country is nothing much out of the ordinary in Great Britain. Modern communications, principally by affordable air travel, have made the world seem smaller through quicker and easier accessibility to most nations. Before the Second World War, when air travel was limited, only the wealthy, or those journeying in the service of their country, crossed the oceans. For most British people even a trip to continental Europe would have been a major event.

Pre-war the majority of people in the provinces had not even visited the national capital and, in some country districts, it was not difficult to find those who had never seen their county town. To many a visitor from another country was, understandably, a considerable curiosity, often being viewed with suspicion; a not unnatural reaction in rural communities where people from a village a few miles distant were often actually referred to as "foreigners". Even so, Britain with its Empire and Commonwealth was probably less insular than most other nations of that pre-war period.

The Second World War of 1939-45 brought to Britain dramatic changes of contact with foreigners. There were the men of the enemy-occupied countries – Poles, Czechs, French, Belgians, Dutch, Norwegians and Danes – who escaped to the United Kingdom to carry on the fight. Also the Commonwealth contingents, predominantly Canadians, but with considerable numbers of Australians, New Zealanders and South Africans, plus those from the colonies. Strange accents were heard and distinguishing shoulder flashes were seen in ever-increasing numbers, but in localised areas. Then, on 7th December 1941, the United States was brought into hostilities and during the following four years some two million American service personnel passed through the UK. This was not only the largest number of combatants from another country to enter these shores up to that time, it was also the first mass coming together of the ordinary people of the United States and the United Kingdom.

Only in the remote parts of northern England and the mountains of Wales and Scotland was the United States serviceman a rare visitor during that period. Elsewhere the GI, the generic term for all US servicemen, was commonplace and in many localities outnumbered the indigenous population 50 to 1. This friendly invasion, through the sheer volume of newcomers, had a marked effect on much of British society. And in many isolated country villages this presence was undoubtedly the most extraordinary happening in their history. At least, it has left a legend that has become almost folklore in some parts of Britain.

If comparatively few Britons had met an American before the Second World War, the reverse was also true. The United States, with approaching forty times the land mass but only four times the population of the UK, had many settlements far more remote than any place in Britain. Many of the young men volunteering or conscripted into the US services had not travelled widely in their own country but the distances between communities found a relatively higher proportion of the population mobile by automobile and railroad. There was not only a much higher proportion of automobiles (the term car did not come into general use until much later in the USA) to people than in the UK; they were affordable – albeit secondhand – by blue collar workers, particularly in rural areas.

Although the United States was still climbing out of the depression years, the ordinary American generally had a much higher standard of domestic comfort than was to be found in British homes. Refrigerators and electrical appliances were in use that were still luxuries in most British homes. The low paid in America, away from those in city tenements, had larger homes than British workers in comparable employment. As an example, a freight locomotive engineer in the US might live in a spacious detached, wood-built house of three or four rooms plus a bathroom.

He would have a second or third-hand automobile and the ability to save some money after purchasing essentials. His equivalent in Britain, a goods engine driver, probably lived in a terraced house with two up and two down, providing half the living space of the American accommodation. No bathroom (under half the houses in the UK had bathrooms in 1939) and a sewered outside toilet would also be the norm. If he lived in the country the toilet was unlikely to be flushed or sewered. The British railwayman would certainly have had less to spend after seeing to the household bills.

Of course, in both countries there were extremes of wealth and poverty, the idle and the industrious. However, the pioneering spirit still pervaded much of American society insomuch as a considerable proportion of the population, particularly from central and eastern Europe, had only arrived during the late nineteenth and early twentieth century and still had the challenge of making good in their new homeland. Enterprise and resourcefulness were admired traits and, generally, a man was assessed on his achievements and acquisitions regardless of his background. Class distinction, which was a marked feature of British society, did not exist to anywhere near the same degree.

Prior to 1939 the divisions of class in Britain were particularly marked. There was an acceptance of one's place in society, a reluctance to transgress on another, and resentment of those who infringed. Breeding, position and wealth were the general yardsticks of class, although the aristocracy would never truly accept a self-made millionaire from humble background as their equal. Even so, the working class man who had become wealthy usually dissociated himself from his origins, seeking only to associate with those of the class he aspired to embrace. Snobbery and inverted snobbery were a familiar part of the British scene.

Of the two nations, the United States was the more insular. Throughout the inter-war period the US government had been at pains to stress its neutrality and disinclination to become involved internationally. In consequence, home affairs were the dominant feature of the news media and the mass of the population were decidedly introverted. The average American citizen neither knew nor cared much for what went on outside his state and, at most, his country. As to what he or she knew of Great Britain, this was to a large extent based on impressions gained during school days. The US language being English, British classics predominated in literature classes, so helping to convey a picture of a somewhat archaic society remote from the American experience, an impression enhanced by Hollywood movies that pursued such legends as Robin Hood, Knights of the Round Table, or some colourful English monarch. And, of course, for the average American, the British were the bad guys who had been booted out in 1776 and Britain was one of the European powers Uncle Sam had had to rescue in the First World War.

British citizens, on the whole, knew more about the United States than the average American knew about their country. Apart from Britain's world-wide commitments and focus on international events, several large American companies had acquired manufacturing facilities in the UK. Ford, General Motors, Kelloggs, Heinz, Hoover and Mars were just a few of the famous names and products that became very familiar in Britain and gave some insight into American ways. But the most influential medium was entertainment. A high proportion of popular melodies broadcast by the BBC stemmed from composers on the other side of the Atlantic and the lyrics made many American place names, features and phrases well known among those who listened to or sang them. Even more influential was the cinema where Hollywood predominated. American film stars like Clark Gable, Katharine Hepburn, Fred Astaire, Ginger Rogers, Edward G. Robinson and a score of others were known in most households. Understandably, the subjects most commonly explored by Hollywood tended to give British filmgoers the impression that, while right always triumphed over wrong, the gun was law, whether it be in the cities or the wild west. Ask a Briton to name one American type character and the chances were that he would answer – the cowboy. There was also a suspicion that with the slightest encouragement an American would burst into a song and dance routine or, at least, that this was a much prized accomplishment in the USA. Over all, Hollywood movies painted a picture of life in the USA being bigger and brighter than in Britain.

The cinema provided escapism for many from the hard-working life in pre-Second World War Britain. A 5½ day working week was normal with holidays taken as unpaid leave. Not all could afford a holiday away, but many managed a visit to the nearest seaside town as the event of the year. Following the outbreak of hostilities in September 1939 came the various discomforts imposed on the nation, particularly rationing. While rationing and other controls did bring a certain social fairness, everyday living gradually became more drab and demanding. So many domestic requisites, once plentiful, became unobtainable or at best in short supply due to the war effort. Make do and mend was a catchphrase and a necessity. The most significant contrast between the United States and Great Britain when both nations became allies in war was the former being, comparatively, the land of plenty while the reverse was the case with the latter.

Whereas a young Briton would distance himself from the children, the American would make them his ally. This fortunate lad is pictured here with ace Lt Colonel Dave Schilling, Air Executive of the 56th Fighter Group at Halesworth. (Tony Kerrison)

2 THE YANKS ARE COMING

IN A MORE limited way, there had been a friendly invasion of Americans into the British Isles during the First World War. The United States declared war on Germany in April 1917 and well over a million American servicemen crossed the Atlantic, mainly to France for the Western Front.

An aviation mission of 12 officers and 93 men from American factories arrived at Liverpool 26th June 1917. Arrangements were made for US Air Service personnel to be given ground trade training at British stations, schools and depots, to a peak of 15,000 at any one time. However, 542 American cadets received flying instruction in the UK and with depot and staff personnel there were 765 officers and 19,307 enlisted men of the US Air Service in the UK by the time of the Armistice, November 1918. By course rotations it is estimated some 31,000 US Air Service men served in Britain 1917-19. Training officially ceased on 5th March 1919. From that date RAF Wyton, near Huntingdon, became the main American holding base in the UK and this closed early in 1920.

The US Navy opened five air stations in Ireland and two, at Eastleigh and Killingholme, in England. Eastleigh, near Southampton, was the depot for the US Marine Northern Bombing Group and from Killingholme in Lincolnshire US Navy pilots flew patrols in Curtiss type flying boats from February 1918 and took over the station from 20th July 1918 until the end of that year. The US complement of the station was around 750 officers and men.

Following The Great War, as it was then known, the United States returned to a policy of neutrality. The common view held was that Uncle Sam had been called upon to get the Europeans out of a mess. In Britain the equally jaundiced notion was that the US had waited until the hard fighting was over before becoming involved. Severe economic depressions preoccupied both nations during the following two decades and although the dictatorial regimes in Italy and Germany did not bode well for peace, the US government pursued a fairly strict isolationist policy. Not until the election of Franklin D. Roosevelt to the Presidency was there a notable change in direction and some measures, although small, to re-arm.

As Hitler began his annexation of European states, US government concern grew as to the eventual aspirations of the fascist dictator. There was a growing moral support for Britain and France, the allies of the Great War, and a willingness to sell them the arms so urgently required. When France fell and Britain was alone, Lend Lease became a lifeline offered by America. With Roosevelt's encouragement the Act authorised the US government to finance and produce war materials and equipment to lease to Britain or other friendly powers. Some commentators in the United States thought Britain's position hopeless and considered such support merely marred the relations with the Axis powers who had established themselves as the dominant European force with which the US might have to come to terms, like it or not. While the majority of its citizens did not want to become involved in another European conflict, several hundred US nationals volunteered to serve with the British forces, notably the Royal Air Force. Their motives varied, with a taste for adventure and a desire to fly combat the most common. The RAF promoted special so-called Eagle Squadrons in Fighter Command for those volunteers trained as fighter pilots but there were nearly as many who flew with other commands.

During 1941 the US increased its support for Great Britain in many ways by taking measures that did not fall far short of a military alliance. In the summer of that year US troops garrisoned Iceland on the pretext of defending the "western hemisphere"; and US experts and engineers, many being military in civilian clothes, were to be found in the UK assisting British forces. This US presence in the UK, supposedly a secret, was soon known to German Intelligence, if not its full extent. Most were in Ulster where the US eventually planned to set up military establish-ments, primarily to police the north Atlan-tic. As in Iceland, British forces were released for service elsewhere. However, on 7th December 1941 Japan attacked the US naval base at Pearl Harbor in the Hawaiian islands and four days later Germany and Italy backed up their Far Eastern ally by declaring war on the United States. Hitler, already having made the fatal mistake of believing his force could defeat the USSR with its vast territory and population, added to his assured demise by this measure, for the Americans and British quickly agreed to "beat Germany first". It would take several months for America's huge industrial capacity to be fully turned to war produc-tion and the manpower trained to provide the forces needed to achieve victory, but as many reasoned authorities observed, the Axis' defeat was now eventually assured.

Northern Ireland remained the immedi-ate planned destination for US military personnel and the first uniformed men arrived six weeks after their country became involved in hostilities. The initial increment, part of the 34th Infantry Div-ision, sailed from New York on 18th January 1942, docking at Belfast on the 26th. The arrival of the GIs was given full publicity, a welcome boost to British morale when most war news was depress-ing. Other shipments of troops were to follow and on 5th February the US Navy formally established a base at London-derry, although its ships had already been using the port.

Landings were soon extended to main-land Britain, although not on a large scale until the spring of 1942. At that time a rapid build-up was under way for a proposed invasion of the European main-land in the autumn of that year. As the weeks went by it became increasingly evident that this would be premature. In mid-June the venture was postponed in favour of landings in north-west Africa, to open a second front to aid the British in the Middle East with the eventual object of ejecting the Axis from that area. Much of the US military strength in Britain was to be used in this campaign, both army and air forces. Of the near 100,000 men who had arrived in the UK by the date for the launch of the invasion in early November 1942, only around 35,000 remained –

largely air force – by the end of the year. Most shipments of troops across the Atlan-tic in the months following the north African invasion were destined for that war zone and not until the following spring was there a substantial rise in the number of American servicemen reaching the UK. By far the greatest influx was to come during the winter and early spring of 1944 with the establishment of the armies and air forces required for entry into Europe. For many of these soldiers their time in Britain was short, for some only a few days, and few combat troops were present for more than nine months.

While the US Army had facilities and camps throughout England and Wales, the main concentration was in Wiltshire and neighbouring counties during the 1943 build-up. By early the following year the sheer volume of soldiers arriving had spread US Army units far and wide, until the immediate pre-invasion deployment to south-western counties. At the time of D-Day, 6th June 1944, there were some 1,600,000 young American servicemen in the UK at more than 1,200 locations.

Following the Normandy invasion the numbers declined at a much sharper rate than they had accumulated until by the autumn air force personnel predominated. There continued to be many thousands of US Army ground forces men and women in the UK through to the end of hostilities, mostly in support organisations such as Services of Supply. A variety of instal-lations ranging from storage depots to hospitals continued to operate long after Germany's defeat.

It was the United States Army Air Forces that had the most permanent association with the UK during the Second World War and whose members, generally, made the most impression on the British populace. Some Air Force men not only served in the UK for more than three years, but at the same location. Moreover, by June 1944, the USAAF had near two-thirds of its total operational combat strength located in England, comprised in terms of men and aircraft of the two largest air forces in history. The vanguard of these vast organisations which would have the longest and most significant presence on the British scene, arrived in London on 20th February 1942. It consisted of Briga-dier General Ira Eaker and his six staff officers with a mission to prepare the way and liaise with the RAF. The USAAF was semi-autonomous with a headquarters in Washington DC, whose commander, General "Hap" Arnold, was only answerable to US Army Chief of Staff, General George Marshall and the higher echelons of the War Department.

In the UK Major General James E. Chaney was, initially, in overall charge of both ground and air forces elements. His selection undoubtedly resulted from his good standing with the British, gained while acting as a military observer in England before the US came into the war. It was Chaney's Aide, Lt Colonel Townsend Griffiss, who on 15th February 1942, became the first USAAF airman to die in line of duty in Europe. He was a passenger in an RAF transport mistakenly

shot down by Polish Spitfire pilots on that date. The USAAF headquarters at Bushy Park, Teddington, was later named Camp Griffiss in his honour.

While it would be several weeks before the first American air tactical units arrived and many more before they were ready to enter combat operations, a few USAAF officers were already gaining experience with RAF squadrons. One of these, Major Cecil Lessig, became the first USAAF pilot to fly on an operational combat mission when, on 25th March 1942, he flew a Spitfire of No 64 Squadron, RAF, on a fighter sweep over the French coast.

The air element of the American military presence was to be designated the 8th Air Force and in April General Eaker established its Bomber Command head-

Airfields built to take bombers and transport aircraft were mostly to British Air Ministry Class A standard. Typical is Langar, Nottinghamshire, which was used by a 9th Air Force troop carrier group. Three intersecting runways, the main 6,000 feet, were encircled by a perimeter track along which were dispersed standings for aircraft, all constructed in concrete. The hutted encampments were dispersed in the neighbouring countryside to lessen damage in the event of an enemy air attack. The communal site with mess halls is at the bottom left of the photograph. (9AF Official)

6

quarters at Wycombe Abbey, a former girls' school just outside the town of High Wycombe, not far from RAF Bomber Command's HQ. The first large consignment of unit personnel for the 8th Air Force sailed from Boston in convoy for Britain on 27th April 1942 in the SS *Andes*, docking at Liverpool on 11th May. The 1,800 men, largely administrative and service personnel, were sent on to airfields at Grafton Underwood, Northants and Molesworth, Huntingdonshire, in an area the Air Ministry had earmarked for the USAAF. Two days later a smaller shipment of USAAF men docking at Newport, Wales, included air crews of the 15th Bomb Squadron, the first flying unit to arrive. With no aircraft of its own, the squadron trained with RAF light bomber squadrons equipped with Douglas Bostons, similar to the A-20 aircraft the 15th had flown before going overseas. The large consignment of USAAF personnel arriving in the Clyde on 10th June aboard the *Queen Elizabeth*, was the first of the regular trans-Atlantic crossings by the two Cunard Queen liners with American servicemen, bringing between 14,000 and 18,000 at a time.

Originally the 8th Air Force was to support the proposed invasion of the European continent but with the substitution of the plan to land in North Africa it was tasked with forming a new air force, the 12th, to support that campaign. Most of the 8th's combat units were to be transferred to the offspring air force and there was hurried action during the summer of 1942 to gain a high state of operational training and, if possible, to give these units some combat experience. Apart from combat, flying would inevitably claim lives in the many accidents that were a feature of those times. The first USAAF airman to become a fatality in such circumstances was 1st Lt Alfred Giacomini who crashed his Spitfire while landing at Atcham, Shropshire, which had become an American fighter training base. On the same day, 29th June 1942, the first bombs were dropped on enemy occupied Europe by USAAF flyers when the CO of the 15th Bomb Squadron, Captain Charles Kegelmen, and his crew flew one of the Bostons of No 226 Squadron RAF, attacking Hazebrouck marshalling yards in France.

The first true operation by the 15th Bomb Squadron, on 4th July, involved six crews flying Bostons with an RAF force attacking airfields in the Netherlands. Two of the American manned aircraft failed to return to Swanton Morley, Norfolk, from which they had taken off. The 8th Air Force's initial offensive operation was pointedly a flag-waving venture for Independence Day, if also a sobering result with six airmen missing in action for little hurt to the enemy. It was with its heavy bombers that the 8th Air Force would determinedly assail Hitler's Fortress Europe commencing the following month.

From the 24 USAAF officers and enlisted men who were present in the UK in April 1942, the total had climbed to 50,000 in six months, only to fall back to around 30,000 by the end of the year due to the North African commitment. Not until the following April did the numbers of US airmen start to climb rapidly, passing the 100,000 mark in June 1943 and doubling by the end of that year. With the establishment of the 9th Air Force, to support the cross-Channel invasion, the numbers accelerated to a peak of 436,000 USAAF personnel in the UK by June 1944. Thereafter the number steadily reduced as the 9th Air Force and many service support organisations transferred to liberated areas of the Continent. Even so, USAAF strength in the UK was still over 200,000 at the European war's end in May 1945.

The largest concentration of USAAF installation was in the greater East Anglian area, where all but a few of the long-term 8th Air Force airfields were located. The 9th Air Force had some presence to the north and south of the East Anglian area but most of its forward airfields were strung out along the south coast. Many supply and support installations were in the Midlands, with major depots at Burtonwood and Warton in Lancashire and also at Langford Lodge in Ulster. During the crowded period before D-Day several 9th Air Force units, noticeably airfield defence anti-aircraft artillery, were spread along the north Norfolk coast and on the border area coast of England and Scotland. All told there were 330 installations other than airfields in use by the USAAF at some time or another during the war and 175 different airfields had a full, part or token USAAF presence.

Men of the 94th Fighter Squadron marching from Ringwood station to Ibsley, c. 27 August 1942. The wearing of steel helmets suggests that a few GIs had taken seriously the rumours of frequent air raids on the southern counties of England. (Ken Sumney)

From the broad highways of his Hollywood, California, home to driving on the left side of the narrow winding English roads must have been a demanding change for Sgt Charles Slater, driver of this light truck. A flock of sheep or herd of cows was a common occurrence, even on major roads. This is the A134 at Sicklesmere, just south of Bury St Edmunds, on 13 December 1943.

Many villages, such as Connington, Huntingdonshire, were literally in the midst of airfield camps.

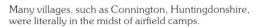

3 THEM AND US

AT AROUND 1.30 pm on a chill spring day early in 1942, two uniformed men emerged from Wright's restaurant in Colchester High Street where refreshment had been taken. They immediately drew attention from passers-by who, used as they were to strange uniforms, had seen nothing quite like these. Two girls stopped and looked back, one exclaiming to the other in tones of awe: "Crumbs, look at his lovely pink trousers!" These two officers were probably the first members of the USAAF seen in this East Anglian town, possibly on an inspection of the numerous airfields being built in the area, whose eventual occupants would make the American serviceman a very common encounter for the local populace.

The early American servicemen were objects of curiosity and their arrival in a new locality received far more interest than had been shown to other nationalities. When the 689th Quartermaster Company arrived at Wickstead Park near Kettering in May 1942, a regular audience of passers-by appeared on the road outside the boundary fence on most evenings and at weekends. These were the locals out for a walk or cycle ride with the object of getting a look at the newcomers. The same thing was to be observed at many installations where Americans were sta-

tioned, arrival invariably bringing many spectators who ambled past taking sly glances, it not being the done thing in British society to openly stop and stare. When asked, one man who had taken a look could only comment with a distinct note of disappointment, "Well, they don't seem much different to ours." When Americans were permitted to leave camp and venture into the local community more realistic appraisals resulted.

On the other side curiosity was not so muted, although GIs had been warned of the famous British reserve and that just because a person in your vicinity did not speak to you it was no indication of unfriendliness. It was suggested that in a small island with such a large population individual privacy could only be respected by not intruding into another person's life without invitation. Many US servicemen noticed that when travelling on the railway it was quite normal to complete the journey without any of the other passengers saying a word to them or anyone else. If, on the other hand, the GI asked a question or made a comment, those addressed were usually more than willing to engage in friendly conversation. Hathy Veynar, one of the first WACs (Women's Army Corps) to reach the UK, encountered this reserve:

> "At first English people seemed reserved and to avoid contact with us, but once the ice was broken they could not have been more friendly and helpful. Introductions were the problem. Mine came when we were putting on a show and wanted some civilian clothes for our girls and boys to wear on the stage. There was a canteen run by a women's voluntary organization at Blackfriars Hall, Norwich, and I went down with the hope that someone could help me. The middle-aged lady I approached said she had a trunk at home full of old clothes and if there was something there we could use she'd be pleased to let us have it. So I got my driver to take us to her house. Evelyn Thwaits became a good friend and thereafter I was often invited to her home. Our relationship lasted until she died."

London bound. Enlisted men of the 100th Bomb Group waiting for a train at Diss station, August 1943. Good creases indicate that best uniforms have been well pressed, but several have the "pants" bottoms turned up. Early issues that fitted at the waist were invariably too long in the leg.

Of course, not all Britons were in the stereotype mould, as Tom Morrow, Ordnance Officer at the 1st Bomb Wing discovered on his first visit to London:

"Some time was allowed for my first look around a little of London. On a stroll up Regent Street a rather touching minor event occurred. Of course, I was in uniform and a rather small, neatly dressed lady of probably some 70 years young accosted me with, 'You're American, aren't you?'
I replied in the affirmative.
'You don't realize how happy we are to see you, you have been missing since the last war and we really do need you!'"

Children were also less inhibited. One officer was amused when a small boy approached him and asked: 'Mister, are your GIs or G1s? My dad wants to know.' The popular term for US servicemen was derived from the initials with which their equipment was frequently stamped – GI for Government Issue.

The general pre-conceived idea the British public had about Americans was that they were big talkers and boastful, a reflection of the flamboyant statements by some uncautioned US dignitaries reported in the press and, to some extent, the images presented by Hollywood that had acknowledged and isolated this tendency. Behind this unsubstantiated view of the big talking American lay more than a tinge of jealousy and resentment that big cousin had come to take over, even if in their heart of hearts they agreed with Winston Churchill that ". . . to have the United States at our side was to me the greatest joy . . ."

There were, of course, those Britons who were already enthusiasts for the United States for numerous reasons, but to many of the younger generation that nation appeared a land of greater opportunity and advancement, again largely through the picture presented by Hollywood and commercial advertising. Even so, there were still people who had not really accepted that the USA was much different in status from Canada, South Africa or other detachments from Empire. Elenor Fredericks, another member of the first WAC increment to arrive in England, encountered an example of this:

"One English lady I got into conversation with when I was walking down town was very enthusiastic about the United States. She said she had told her children that after

The choice of either "olives" or "pinks" (the "pinks" were truly a pinkish fawn) could be worn with an officer's standard olive tunic. These men of 351st Bomb Group were taking a trip on Loch Lomond during a furlough in September 1944. (l. to r. T. Cooper, F. Williams, S. Taylor and R. Johnson). (Thomas Cooper)

the war America was where they should go; there was a better future in the colonies! I said nothing."

Prejudice was to be found among some US servicemen; chiefly those believing that Britain should still be seen as the enemy of 1776; or first-generation stock whose parents had come from continental Europe and perpetuated the suspicion of the offshore islands; but mostly those Irish-Americans – more Irish than the Irish themselves – conditioned into believing that Britain was still the persecutor of Ireland; distrust that often endured but happily was mostly muted or dissolved through personal contacts with the British. There were, of course, those who through persuasion or experience came to dislike the British people and continued to do so. One of the most distinguished fighter pilots is on record as saying that during his time with the 8th Air Force he did not know who he hated most, the Germans or the British. And there are many GIs' diaries that record disenchantment, invariably because of the unfriendly attitude they perceived or a failure to understand that in many respects the British were not like Americans. Despite explanations about British attitudes and the so-called reserve, most GIs' dislike continued to be generated by what they took to be the "cold shoulder", an unfriendly attitude, particularly so with those they came to recognise as middle and upper class.

Another, not uncommon view, was that the British were beset with apathy and given to complaining, yet did not appear

Wartime Britain was shabby, the houses often in a poor state of upkeep. In really rural areas piped water and sewered sanitation were rare. Each cottage had its well or was served by a village pump. "Kinda quaint" in the view of many GIs, like these men from the 303rd Bomb Group watching a Spaldwick woman fill her pail.

The same house a near half century later. The village pump long gone and the thatched barn rebuilt with tiled roof. (Quenton Bland)

The typical GI UK home. Lt Royal Snell outside the Nissen hut occupied by the eight officers of two heavy bomber crews at Lavenham, Suffolk. Every man had a cycle (one a woman's model). (Royal Snell)

Mud was enemy No 1 at most USAAF camps. GIs attempt to improve the situation at Seething, Norfolk, by creating drainage basins around the parachute and flight equipment building.

to confront their problems. They had an apparent acceptance of situations which, to American eyes, demanded immediate action. A few US servicemen saw this in a kinder light; Lt Jack Bryant, stationed at Sudbury, Suffolk wrote: "An area of distinct difference would be the Englishman's patience with and the ability to endure periods of hardship while the American, faced with similar circumstances, will tend to be impatient and will take action, not always well designed, but generally decisive, to improve things. At times this is a strength, even though long-term results may not be the most advantageous." There was a common view that the British were lazy, in the majority of cases based on the slowness of those civilian workmen on US military establishments. The frequency of "tea breaks" and the lethargy observed led to these individuals becoming a joke. When one unmindful labourer was struck and killed by the propeller of a manoeuvring Liberator at Hethel airfield, its ground crew painted a small tea cup and saucer symbol on the aircraft's "scoreboard". The station headquarters were quick to have this ill-placed humour removed but, although a tragedy, the incident remained a source of humour for many US servicemen at that base.

While many of the civilians employed on USAAF bases were industrious and gave good service, the American view was to some extent justified, for such employment was well known in British circles as attracting those who wanted an easy time. Moreover, the construction labourers, a large proportion of whom were Irish, were in no hurry to work themselves out of well paid employment, an aspect not readily appreciated by US personnel frustrated by the slow pace of completing their installations.

To a large proportion of American servicemen the British were inferior beings. This was not so much a conscious appraisal, but an automatic assumption by the average GI's belief that the USA was God's own country, an expression of that introverted national pride on which US citizens were reared. The majority found Britain rather archaic, a confirmation of what they had surmised from schooling in English literature, bolstered by personal observations of the social and domestic scene where the US was certainly more advanced. In consequence British people

were taken to be a little old fashioned and disadvantaged. "Kinda quaint, like the place," as one GI observed.

A final reason for disdain centred upon personal hygiene. "I have to admit that the thing that struck me most after my first journey on an English bus was the smell. It stank and so did the people," a Washington man recalled. Such was the reputation of the British for being smelly that behind their backs they were referred to as "goats" and England as "Goatland" at some bases. In the continental climate of the United States where many areas have summer temperatures well over 100F degrees, showering and bathing were almost a necessity of life, even in the poorest households. In the temperate UK with a preponderance of cold, damp weather, much of the population did not feel the need or have the facilities for regular immersion in water. For half the population a movable tin bathtub served the purpose, usually once a week. With wartime restriction on fuel for heating water and the rationing of soap, bathing became an even more difficult proposition and for those disinclined to personal hygiene the excuse to have no more than a good wash. Women were more particular but a goodly number of British men were not for close company during the war years.

American characteristics or habits to which the British took an aversion became well known. The preconceived notion of boastfulness was confirmed for many citizens by their observations of, and superficial contacts with GIs. What failed to be appreciated was that an American's tendency to talk about his achievements and possessions was not seen as bragging in his homeland but as an accepted way to establish one's worth and status in society. It was a form of openness and only censured if the claims were untrue. Nevertheless, to the British it appeared "bad form" by their own standards. It would be false to suggest that all GIs projected themselves in this way; there were many who were quite as reticent as the average Briton.

Understandably, to the generally disciplined and reserved nation they had "invaded", the GI appeared impudent if not ill mannered. Often there was no hesitation in the GI introducing himself to a complete stranger, particularly a girl.

The GI was a magnet where kids were concerned. When Sgt Philip Moose sat down with his water colours to paint a boatyard scene at Wivenhoe, Essex, he soon had a dozen spectators. (Robert Sand)

No. 93587

PASSED BY 19764 U S ARMY EXAMINER CENSORS STAMP

Dr. O. A. Sand
311 Whatcom St.
Bellingham, Wash.
U.S.A.

Sgt R. T. Sand
SENDERS NAME
38th Fighter Sqdn.
SENDERS ADDRESS
A.P.O. 637 N.Y. N.Y.
Sept. 19, 1943
DATE

Hello Folks!
Well, here I am in good old England! (Somewhere) It's wonderful! Sure hope you haven't worried, because I am enjoying this immensely. I'll admit I'm not stuck on English cooking, but I sure like their tea, and a combination porridge and pudding they make. Strange as it may seem, I find their bitters (beer) very easy to drink. The English people are wonderful to us, tho, as a whole, I don't think we deserve it. I couldn't begin to describe the beautiful, antique towns, villages, thatched roof cottages, and all. Much more of it than I expected to find. The first little country pub I visited was a little thatched affair with hand hewed oak beams, (with an old barkeep right out of Dumas) that has stood for at least 600 years! Think of it! And these blackouts! It's amazing to walk thru noisy, crowded streets, and see nothing but shadows and darkness. Right away I met some Vancouver, B.C. boys who have been here from a year and a half to three years. I haven't received any mail yet, but will soon. Write some V-mail, some regular. Say hello to all. Hope you're all fine.
Love,
Bob

V ~ MAIL

A first letter from England. (Robert Sand)

V-Mail became the reference to all letters from home, although this term originally applied to a printed form airmail, photographically reduced to enable more to be carried in the limited air traffic across the Atlantic. These men on a Snetterton Heath site hope for a letter from home, one of the biggest morale lifters for any man separated from his family.

What was brashness to British eyes would be nothing untoward in US everyday society, although being in a foreign country, like all young servicemen abroad, the GI was less restrained by considerations of demeanour than in his own land.

Another accusation voiced by the British was that the average GI was slovenly and did not comport himself as a soldier should. Indeed, in comparison with the men of a European army, the off-duty GI was often remarkably casual about his appearance. A view of high command was that their soldiers were present to fight a war and not to conduct parades. Even so, there were commanders who took a tougher line. One was Brigadier General "Monk" Hunter who headed VIIIth Fighter Command at Bushey Hall, Watford. Always immaculately dressed and deporting himself in the best military manner, he abhorred slovenliness. Soon after his headquarters was set up he received an extremely large pre-war British civilian limousine for use as a staff car until an American vehicle became available. While being driven in this limousine to some appointment he chanced to see a number of his enlisted men waiting for either taxis or a bus outside the main gate. All had hands in pockets, some had tunics undone and a few slouched against a fence. Hunter was so incensed he ordered his driver to stop so that he could go back and remonstrate with the offenders. When the limousine came to a stop, the waiting GIs, not recognising it, apparently thought that some kind British civilian was offering a lift. There being more than the limousine could take, a mad rush ensued to be first in. We have no record of what the General said when the men tried to scramble in but they must have received a considerable shock on seeing who the occupant was.

Uniform was a great leveller and the nature and background of the person it clothed not evident to a British contact through manner, speech and other behaviour as it was to another American. As would have been the case with British or troops of other nationalities, military service in a foreign land provided opportunities for the "out for a good time" extroverts to behave in a manner that they would not have entertained in their own land. Their prominence in Britain's villages and towns was, understandably, the basis for the natives' opinions of US servicemen. The thousands of quiet, orderly young men were overlooked in these generalised assessments. Perhaps the administrative officer of a US fighter station was grossly exaggerating when he informed a farmer friend that "half the enlisted men on this base were hoboes before the war" but it is worth remembering that many GIs, to use a favourite American catchphrase of the time, never had it so good.

Eventually an understanding and acceptance developed among host and visitors. Americans came to respect the stoicism and quiet endurance of their ally; the British to admire the resourcefulness and gaiety of the GI and to note the open sentimentality of these young men in contrast to their own presentation of the "stiff upper lip".

"You can always tell a Yank 'cause his stripes are upside down". The jacket in this GI wardrobe at Bassingbourn is that of a Technical Sergeant, two bars below the chevrons. The Fortress radio operator to whom it belonged had just gone Missing In Action when the photograph was taken in June 1943.

US officers' uniforms were extremely smart. In so-called Ike jackets and pink pants, Lieutenants Lou Ades (left) and Preston Red pose outside their barracks at Hethel. Both men have "crushed hats", the mark of a combat flier. (Louis Ades)

As the district police sergeant I was informed by Divisional Office to expect Americans at Kings Cliffe railway station and to go along and see that there were no problems. It was a cold January afternoon in 1943. I drove up and was surprised to find a number of American soldiers already in the station yard. They turned out to be members of a brass band who had been driven up from some headquarters to provide welcoming music for the troops arriving by train. I hadn't been there long when another American vehicle arrived with a doughnut making machine on board. I'd never seen anything like this. The operators immediately set about turning out doughnuts and handing them around to the bandsmen and the villagers who had come to see what was going on.

It was dark before the troop train finally arrived. These fellows had only been in this country a few hours, having come straight off a ship in the Clyde. A very strong wind was blowing and as it passed under the station building, which was raised on stilts, it made a howling noise. One of the newly arrived officers asked how close we were to the sea and I said "not far", meaning about 30 miles. Then I realised that he and the others thought the noise made by the wind was the sea; they thought that with a name like Kings Cliffe they were somewhere right on the coast. These fellows may have been tired but they cannot have been that tired because the following morning I received a call and was told two cases of scotch whisky had been stolen from the station. It was arranged for me to meet a railway policeman and together we went to the airfield. To our surprise the administrative officer we were taken to see was walking around wearing his medals. He had obviously seen service elsewhere and wanted us to know. We did recover a few empty bottles from the camp cinema but that was all. I suspect the Americans weren't particularly anxious to find the guilty party, probably thinking the warming celebration of their arrival at Kings Cliffe was justified.

Jack Neasham

I was detached from the FANY to act as a driver for officers of the US Army Services of Supply at Cheltenham. Stayed with them three years. They were enormous fun to be with, very friendly, clued up, yet there was a simple naturalness about them. I think most were still civilians at heart.

While they did not expect you to take their remarks at face value, it was important to know that one should never make jokes about their flag or national institutions. On the other hand, some were not too careful in what they said about us. On one occasion the officer I was driving actually said they had come over to win the war for us. I was so cross I stopped the car and ordered him out. He got out, but by then I had calmed down enough to appreciate the situation of having ordered a US officer out of a US vehicle. Fortunately, he apologised and I relented and let him resume his seat!

Daphne Chute

Even places of worship were made available for use by US services. The parish church at Cranford, Northants, was turned over to local USAAF on Thursday 23 November 1944 when Protestant padre, Major Ward Fellows, conducted a Thanksgiving Service. (Vic Maslen)

I had finished my last combat mission and was given a seven day pass. I hitched a ride on a weapons carrier to Halesworth railway station to catch the London train. I bought my ticket and was going toward the train on the wrong side for proper boarding as it started to move out of the station. There was a track between me and the London train with another train approaching on it. I was 20, and had seen several movies of people catching moving trains. I quickly crossed the track, tossed my bag in an open window, jumped up and started thru after it. I had my head, shoulders and one leg inside with both hands on the window ledge. A young limey in civvies put his hands on my shoulders, pushed me backward and said, "You can't come in here!"

"Why not?" I demanded.

He said, "Because there are women and children in here."

I noticed it was a larger compartment than usual, there were several people therein including a lady with a baby in a stroller.

He repeated, "You can't come in!"

I looked out the window at the oncoming train and wondered if there would be clearance between it and me.

I said, "OK! Throw my bag off."

I jumped down, bounded over the tracks just ahead of the train. It must have missed by inches! That Englishman nearly did what the Germans couldn't do in 32 missions: kill me!

Whenever I tell this story someone asks, "Why didn't you slug the SOB?" I often wonder about the many possibilities the conversation between the people in that compartment may have taken during the rest of the trip.

Ivan Brown

The "pot-bellied stove" provided for Nissen hut heating was an exasperating joke. Getting it to light was a work of art – as was keeping it burning. Privates C.M. Link's and Charles Murphy's attempt to bake potatoes by removing the grate was apparently unsuccessful.

4   THE AIR WAR

Dawn 10 December 1944. Looking east from Wormingford, Essex. Each trail headed east is a bomber formation at over 20,000 feet leaving England for another bombing operation over Hitler's *Festung Europa*. The paradox of this scene of war was its extraordinary beauty.   (Robert Sand)

FOR THE majority of British people and the American servicemen in their midst, the strategy of what had come to be called the air war was not comprehended or questioned; it was accepted as a necessary part of the plan to beat Hitler. Perhaps not as simply as the Suffolk farm sage who affirmed: "Tha's like this – Jerry bomb us and they be going to bomb him back ten for every one"; but most individuals' views were shaped by personal experience allied to what was read in newspapers or heard on the radio. In southern and eastern England the volume of noise from aircraft engines was an almost constant reminder of the air war and on clear days the hundreds of specks etching the blue with white condensation trails was a spectacle few could ignore. While it was truly all part of the scheme of things to bring about the defeat of Nazi Germany and its allies, the air war had a deeper significance in that air power in its own right was being put to the test.

The invention of powered flying machines in the early years of this century was quickly seen by generals and admirals as a promising means of being able to observe the disposition of an enemy's armies and fleets. In the First World War the still primitive aircraft would quickly develop to carry and dispense ordnance and with machine gun installations the airmen of opposing aircraft were able to shoot each other out of the sky. A notable recognition of the new form of warfare the aeroplane had introduced came with the creation of a separate service by the British, the Royal Air Force. But for other combatants air operations remained an adjunct of those of army and navy, for while aeroplanes were undoubtedly very useful, they did not seriously influence the outcome of campaigns or the war.

However, the potential of the aeroplane was appreciated by a few military strategists who envisaged fleets of long range-aircraft being able to bomb an enemy's

17

The air war seen from
the ground; formations
of Liberators.
December 1944.

A Thunderbolt preparing for take-off from Thruxton,
Hampshire, on a fighter-bomber raid. Lt H.W. Collins
signals the pilot of each plane when to start his roll.
April 1944.

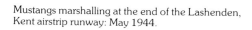

Mustangs marshalling at the end of the Lashenden,
Kent airstrip runway: May 1944.

war production and distribution systems – his arms and munitions factories, fuel supplies, transportation and shipping – so that it would be impossible or at least difficult to pursue a modern war. This concept came to be known as strategic bombing. After the First World War it was fostered by many in the RAF but budgetary restrictions prevented the establishment of such a bombing force until the British government finally awoke to the ambitions of Hitler. The rapid advancement of fighter aircraft design among the European nations led the RAF to believe long range bombing operations in daylight would be untenable. For this reason the British strategic bomber force was built around a pre-conceived necessity to operate under cover of darkness.

The strategic bombing concept was nurtured by several senior officers in the United States Army Air Corps who also saw it as a justification for an autonomous air force. The US Army, traditionalists, would have none of this and it was certainly not germane to the policy of national isolation pursued by US governments for much of the inter-war period. A more enlightened administration under Franklin D. Roosevelt suspected that the US would be drawn into the conflict with Hitler and his acolytes and the events in Europe during 1939-40 brought American acceptance of the need to build a strategic bombing force. While still firmly part of the US Army, its expanding aviation branch was given semi-autonomy in June 1941 with the creation of the US Army Air Forces.

Only Britain and the United States of all the combatant nations were firmly committed to strategic bombing and had developed the means to conduct it. The USAAF's brand was based on a doctrine of high altitude daylight precision bombing. Although the RAF and the Luftwaffe had turned away from daylight bombing raids, senior US air commanders believed they could succeed through technical developments which had been perfected during the latter part of the 1930s. While these had not initially been developed for this specific purpose, their availability made high altitude precision bombing possible. For flight above 10,000 feet oxygen breathing equipment and supply was desirable; above 15,000 feet it was essential. Because of the limitations of

oxygen supply the British, German and other combatants' bombing operations were chiefly conducted at altitudes up to around 15,000 feet. US engineers developed a self-regulatory system that automatically adjusted the oxygen to the demand of the airmen with changes in altitude. The system was efficient at as high an altitude as 30,000 feet. The depleted air at such an altitude also affected aero-engine operations. Without ground level air consistency the correct air-fuel mixture to give maximum power could not be fed to the engines. A turbo-supercharger had been developed which compressed the air to the desired amount enabling maximum power to be sustained at high altitude. Thus it was practical for aircraft fitted with this equipment to operate at altitudes of 25,000 feet and more, where it was believed current fighters would have difficulty in reaching and anti-aircraft artillery would either fall short or be inaccurate. The viability of this concept was further encouraged by the fact that the early Boeing B-17 four-engine bombers used in high altitude experiments proved faster than the US Army fighter interceptors of the time.

The third innovation that brought reality to the high altitude bombing plan was the so-called Norden bombsight. N.L. Norden was a mathematical engineering genius, and in effect he designed an electro-mechanical computer which, when correctly set up, could deliver bombs with great accuracy on a small target from heights of 20,000 feet and more. The bombsight that took his name was far in advance of any others designed for a similar purpose and its details were highly secret. With data on the height and speed of the aircraft, wind direction and velocity, bomb ballistics entered in and the sight aimed on the target, the Norden would automatically release the ordnance at the right moment to achieve a direct hit or a very near miss.

When the evidence of modern fighters' successes against bombers was forthcoming from Europe during the first two years of hostilities, the USAAF turned to installing formidable defensive armament in its medium and heavy bombers – as many as 12 heavy calibre machine guns. It further planned to fly its day bombers in large, close formations, believing that the concentration of firepower forwarded would

An American Fortress bomber stands on its concrete pad in an English gentleman's country park, Goswold Hall, Thrandeston, Suffolk. A view from the main Ipswich-Norwich highway (A140). (Arnold Delmonico)

Overloaded with fuel and bombs, every take-off for war was an anxious time for the nine or ten young men of a heavy bomber crew. If an engine faltered, the loss of power might precipitate a crash. (Arnold Delmonico)

deter or make difficult effective intercep-tion by enemy fighters. Even before the USA was involved in hostilities plans were made for the deployment of United States air forces to the United Kingdom. Similarly the British Air Ministry looked towards the possibility of American involvement in an air campaign against German war industry by surveying and selecting sites for bomber airfields. When, in December 1941, Japan opened the offensive in the Pacific and South-East Asia, and Germany and Italy declared war on the United States, work to establish the proposed bomber force became a top priority. USAAF leaders saw an opportunity to pursue their concept of strategic bombing from the United Kingdom as a prelude to any allied invasion of continental Europe; indeed there were those who believed that a successful campaign alone might bring about Germany's capitulation. At least the situation appeared favourable to test the plans for high altitude daylight

precision bombing since most of German war industry would be within the range of the American heavy bombers. Success would enhance the case for air power. Moreover, a combined bomber offensive wherein the RAF attacked by night and the USAAF by day provided an even better chance of attaining that goal.

The US air force destined for the UK was to consist of no less than 75 bomber groups, one group to an airfield. A group was the main operational bomber organisation for although each had four component squadrons it was a group rather than a squadron that undertook combat missions. To accommodate this force, the British undertook a crash building programme, up to that time the biggest civil engineering feat in the British Isles in terms of the labour and materials involved. Each of the bomber airfields cost over a million pounds (in 1992 it is estimated that the equivalent cost would be near 100 million each) and this construction programme was additional to the provision of many similar airfields for the expansion of RAF Bomber Command. There was also a requirement for 25 airfields for USAAF fighter groups (with three squadrons each) but these did not have to have the hard concrete runways that were essential for the bombers and were thus easier to provide. Also needed were another 20 bases for reconnaissance

and transport units. The plan was to have most of this vast air force, which amounted to some two-thirds of the total American combat air forces, in place by the summer of 1943. This was to prove too ambitious as, due to insufficient trained men, aircraft and airfields, less than half of the force was on hand by the planned date.

The heavy bombers which were to constitute the main force amounted to 60 groups in the original plan, approximately half equipped with the Boeing B-17 Fortress and half with the Consolidated B-24 Liberator. These aircraft were of similar dimensions – a little over 100 feet wingspans – and each powered by four air-cooled engines, with a crew of ten, four officers and six "enlisted men" (NCOs). All but the two pilots on every B-17 or B-24 would combine their main duties with that of gunnery or be a full-time gunner handling the ten or 12 machine guns installed as defensive armament. These weapons were .50-inch calibre, having a higher velocity and – within effective range - much greater destructive power than the rifle calibre machine guns commonly used as defensive armament in British and German bombers. The Fortress's bomb load was normally 4,000-6,000 pounds, dictated by the shape and size of its bomb bay although the aircraft was quite able to lift loads of more than double that weight. The Liberator, a later design with more modern systems, was also handicapped by the dimensions of its bomb bay and could not carry an appreciably larger load. While 4,000-6,000 might look uneconomical compared with the 8,000-12,000 frequently taken to the enemy by RAF Lancasters, it proved heavy enough for transporting in the thin atmosphere five miles above the earth.

Fifteen of the bomber bases planned were for so-called medium types, the North American B-25 Mitchell and the Martin B-26 Marauder, both twin-engined aircraft capable of lifting 3,000 pound bomb loads, but limited to around half the range of the heavies. Their crews numbered six or seven and the armament on some models was as heavy as in the B-17s and B-24s.

USAAF headquarters in the United Kingdom was designated the 8th Air Force and the definitive plan for deployment of this large bomber assembly placed 15 groups (airfields) in an administrative and operational control organisation originally called a Wing and later a Division. The 1st Wing with B-17 Fortresses was to be based on airfields around, but mostly to the west of, Cambridge. The 2nd Wing, flying B-24 Liberators, took airfields in central and south Norfolk, the 3rd Wing was to have a mixture of B-25 Mitchell and B-26 Marauder groups and use bases in Suffolk. The 4th Wing would have B-17s in north Essex and south-east Suffolk; the 5th Wing with B-24s was to be placed on airfields in south and central Essex. However, the contingencies of war and the sheer enormity of the programme embarked upon, brought some changes to the plan. Japanese advances in the Pacific and the critical situation in the Middle East caused the diversion of several groups originally destined for the United Kingdom. Until American forces were fully mobilised and war industry got into full stride, there were shortages of both trained men and equipment.

As related, the USAAF first participated in a combat bombing operation from England on 4th July 1942. The heavy bombers did not go into action until 17th August that year when 12 Fortresses attacked rail yards at Rouen, France. Thereafter the heavy bombers were fairly regularly in action and their numbers were swelled by other groups entering combat. But before it could get into its stride the 8th Air Force was tasked with forming the 12th Air Force, the American air element of the allied forces in the planned invasion of North Africa in November 1942. Apart from the most experienced units being transferred to the 12th, several new groups, originally destined for the 8th, were also sent on to North Africa. For the next six months the heavy bomber campaign was largely carried by four Fortress groups operating from Thurleigh, Bassingbourn, Chelveston and Molesworth. During this period most of the procedures and tactics employed by the 8th Air Force heavy bombers were established and remained little changed for the duration of hostilities.

Preparations for a combat bombing mission at a bomber airfield began during the night with operations and intelligence staff producing the necessary flight plans and target information for pilots, navigators and bombardiers, and issuing details of fuel and bomb loads to the maintenance and ordnance sections. The personnel of combat crews would be awakened about three hours before the scheduled take-off time, going first to breakfast and then to the briefing for the mission. Heavy sheepskin and electrically heated flying suits were donned before transport out to the aircraft.

Mechanics had been pre-flighting their aircraft for several hours before the combat crews arrived, sometimes for most of the night – and they did not eat or sleep until the aircraft had departed. At the pre-arranged time engines would be started and the bombers moved out from their dispersal points onto the airfield perimeter track. Departure was a noisy business with perhaps 25 aircraft – and in later years near double that number - lined one behind the other on the track waiting turn to take off. Each had four 1,200 hp engines running, opened up to full power for take-off. A fully laden Fortress or Liberator required all of a 4,500 ft runway and most of a 6,000 ft runway to obtain the desired speed for a good lift-off – about 120mph. It was an apprehensive time for the crews for they knew that if an engine failed as they left the ground the chances were that the bomber would abruptly return to earth; crashing with bombs and 2,800 gallons of fuel meant an explosion and fire. There was not one 8th Air Force heavy bomber base that did not experience a fatal take-off crash and at most there were several during the course of operations.

The bombers took off at 30-45 second intervals, climbed steadily away from the airfield to a specified area of sky where they orbited while gaining altitude. Aircraft following the leader would shorten their turns so that gradually a formation was assembled: first flights then squadrons and finally group formations of up to 27 aircraft in the early days, but with 36 or more in later months. It took about two hours to assemble and marshal formations and to reach the required altitude, generally about 20,000 ft, before striking out for the sea and enemy territory. The height was necessary to minimize the effects of enemy anti-aircraft fire – flak – on crossing the enemy held coastline.

On clear days the morning departures provided the most extraordinary sight as, often, hundreds of bombers curved through the heavens, their paths marked by the white streaks of vapour trails that quickly expanded into broad bands. The hot engine exhaust mixing with the frigid air at high altitude produced the vapour which in some weather conditions actually persisted to produce an overcast. The aircraft within a squadron formation were staggered up and down and from side to side, while the three squadrons that usually composed a group formation were similarly staggered so that the whole resembled an angled wedge. The object was to give clear fields of fire to as many gun positions as possible and minimize the risk of gunners actually shooting into other bombers in the formation.

Two, three or four groups eventually positioned relative to one another to form a Combat Wing and Combat Wings, separated by a few miles, sallied forth in trail to complete the Divisional Air Task Force. At the appointed time, known as Zero Hour, the force headed out over a prominent landmark, usually a town, on the English coast. Planning times for the mission were all worked out both back and forth from Zero Hour. The duration of the mission obviously depended on the distance to be flown and while an attack on the Ruhr might take only six hours overall, many distant targets demanded flight times of 10 or 11 hours before the

returning bombers landed at base. Once the enemy coast had been re-crossed on withdrawal, formations reduced altitude so that the crews could come off oxygen and to allow the formation to spread out to ease pilots' concentration on keeping close station. When regaining England, the Fortresses and Liberators were down to a few thousand feet and often swept over the countryside towards their bases at not far above church steeple height. The formation was retained until reaching the vicinity of the home base, when squadrons would separate and orbit while the aircraft in each "peeled off" to make a landing approach. Bombers firing two red flares indicated wounded on board and a request for priority to come in first. Often battle damaged – ragged tailplanes, holed wings, feathered (stationary) propellers – were clearly visible to people in the vicinity of an airfield as the bombers returned.

Trucks would pick up the crews at the aircraft dispersal points and take them to the interrogation building. Here, while the men ate doughnuts and drank coffee, intelligence officers would take down details of what befell and what was seen by each crew. After interrogation the men were free to return to their barracks. Even though young – average age of 22 – most were exhausted. The reduced air pressure experienced in high altitude flight made digestive systems uneasy and induced fatigue. Added to this, constant noise – only partially subdued by earphones – the extreme cold, discomfort of wearing an oxygen mask, to say nothing of apprehension and fear, put considerable strain on the strongest of constitutions. As a result many combat men spent much of their non-flying time sleeping. Extreme tiredness was a common post-mission experience.

In the spring of 1943 the 8th Air Force heavy bomber forces build-up began again and new groups arrived in England throughout the summer. Four medium bomber groups equipped with the B-26 Marauder also arrived for the 3rd Wing. The first was initially based at Bury St Edmunds and in May instigated American medium bomber operations with two attacks on a power station in Holland. In contrast to the sub-stratosphere levels of heavy bomber operations, the Marauders went in very low, at "tree top" height. On

Ground crew men view the smoke plume caused by a bomb cluster accidentally released from a P-38 Lightning. Happily it exploded without endangering life in a field near Bures on the Essex/Suffolk border. (Robert Sand)

the second raid all of the 11 aircraft reaching Holland were lost. The Marauder was obviously too large and slow for such a mode of employment and for near two months operations with the type were suspended. In late July the Marauder groups began operating at so-called medium altitudes – 10,000-16,000 ft – in tight formations similar to the heavy bombers. With their main targets airfields in occupied countries, the B-26s proved very successful using the new tactics and, in fact, had a loss per sortie ratio of only .3 per cent whereas the heavy bomber losses were running near 10 per cent at that time.

A heavy bomber crew man had to undertake 25 combat missions before being removed from combat flying – a tour. During 1943 an individual had a 35 per cent chance of completing his tour, that is, only one in three survived. This high rate of attrition was due mostly to Luftwaffe fighters. The massed defensive fire from Fortress formations was not the deterrent once anticipated and although a formidable obstacle, German fighters soon began to develop successful tactics to break up the bomber formations and were at times able to take a heavy toll of the American bombers. Even so, the Fortresses were never once turned back from their targets by the enemy, despite heavy losses.

What did frustrate the 8th Air Force on many occasions was the weather. The ideal of daylight precision bombing had been perfected in the fairly predictable weather conditions of the United States. In north-west Europe the weather was not so co-operative and a succession of weather fronts severely restricted operations. Even when the prognosis favoured clear skies, the bombers could fly perhaps 300 or 400 miles from their bases only to find the target obscured by cloud. The solution was to use the development of the ground scanning radar that RAF Bomber Command employed in its night raids, so that if visual bombing could not be achieved a "blind bombing" attack with the aid of radar could be made on a suitable target.

During the first winter of operations the targets for the 8th Air Force bombers had often been associated with U-boat facilities. In the summer of 1943 the 8th Air Force joined RAF Bomber Command in what was known as the Combined Bomber Offensive with agreed target priorities. Of major importance was the neutralization of the Luftwaffe, for it was obvious that this was the major obstacle to pursuing a comprehensive campaign of strategic bombing. Thus many of the targets attacked by the Fortresses during the summer and early autumn of 1943 were aircraft factories and associated installations. While the original concept of heavily armed bombers being able to fight their way to the target and back had certainly proved feasible, the cost was

Opposite: D-Day plus 4. A squadron of B-26 Marauders assembles its formation under the fading contrails made by the heavies in the purple dawn. (Robert Sand)

Those who never left. Part of the American Military Cemetery at Madingley, Cambridge where 3,812 US service personnel are buried – mostly airmen. The Wall of the Missing contains another 5,125 names of those with no known resting place. (Ian Mactaggart)

becoming prohibitive. Apart from bombers brought down over enemy territory, many that returned to England were damaged beyond economical repair or required considerable work to put them back into commission.

The need for fighter escorts, to hold off the enemy interceptors, was acknowledged earlier that year by three groups, flying Republic P-47 Thunderbolts, starting operations. The Thunderbolt, large by comparison with its adversaries and most other single-seat engine fighters of its day, was about twice the size and weight of a Spitfire. Because of these factors the Thunderbolt had a poor rate of climb, but having a turbo supercharged engine it was as fast as enemy fighters in level flight at

30,000 ft, and in a dive its weight and power usually enabled it to overhaul an adversary. Positioned high above the bombers hey were escorting, the Thunderbolts were frequently able to pounce on Messerschmitts and Focke-Wulfs as they prepared to attack the B-17s or B-24s. The problem was that the Thunderbolt's endurance only enabled it to give escort for a short distance over enemy held territory. With "drop tanks" (disposable fuel tanks) slung under their fuselages, Thunderbolts were able to reach as far as the borders of Germany. Faced with this development the Luftwaffe waited until the escort had to turn back before committing its fighters in force to intercept the American bombers.

In the autumn of 1943 fighter groups equipped with Lockheed P-38 Lightnings began flying escort missions from England. The twin-engined Lightnings were unorthodox in having two boom fuselages linking empennage to wing; although comparatively large aircraft for fighters they were surprisingly manoeuvrable. With two large drop tanks the fighter offered the prospect of affording escort for the heavy bombers to targets as distant as Berlin. Unfortunately, the Lightning had operating problems, the most serious being the frequency with which engines failed due to the high humidity air and extreme cold encountered over north-west Europe at high altitudes.

In the autumn of 1943 two developments further reduced the eventual size of the 8th Air Force. With the cross-Channel invasion of France set for the following spring a large number of air units specifically tasked to support the ground forces were programmed to be sent to the UK before this event. It was decided to create a new American air force for this purpose, the 9th, by taking the appropriate units already assigned to the 8th - the medium bomber Marauders, troop carrier and tactical reconnaissance groups – under a new command headquarters. The second development resulted from the USAAF high command's impatience with what they saw as a slow rate of operations in the strategic bombing campaign due primarily to inclement weather. The Allied invasion of Italy provided airfield sites in the southern part of that country offering an area of better weather with bases nearer to some of the planned objectives. In consequence groups that would have formed the fourth heavy bomber division of the 8th Air Force were sent to Italy to become the new 15th Air Force. However, 8th Air Force headquarters in London was retitled as United States Strategic Air Forces in Europe and had operational control over both the 8th and 15th Air Forces and administrative control of the 9th Air Force.

In the winter of 1943 and the following spring, the size of the 8th Air Force doubled and the 9th Air Force grew from seven to 45 groups. Four more groups equipped with B-26 Marauders began operating from Essex airfields as did three with Douglas A-20 Havoc light bombers. They were targeted on airfields, communication centres and V-1 flying bomb sites in the coastal belt of occupied France and the Low Countries.

The first fighter groups received by the 9th Air Force, based in the Colchester area, provided escort for the bombers of both air forces before moving down to the landing grounds in Kent where their operational commitment gradually changed to fighter-bomber work, attack-ing enemy installations at low-level. By the spring of 1944, 9th Air Force fighter groups were present in several southern counties to as far west as Somerset. Three groups flew the P-38 Lightning but most used the P-47 Thunderbolt which, due to its rugged construction and heavy armament, excelled in attacking ground targets. However, the very first fighter group received by the 9th Air Force was equipped with the new North American P-51 Mustang.

The original Mustang was produced in America for the RAF. Redesigned, to feature a Rolls-Royce Merlin engine, it had an excellent performance but its great advantage over other American fighter types was an inbuilt fuel capacity permitting it to range 400 miles from base. Obviously the Mustang was just what the harassed 8th Air Force heavy bombers needed for escort; following the operational debut of the first unit in December 1943, most Mustangs arriving in the UK went to equip or re-equip the 8th Air Force fighter force. Eventually 14 of its 15 groups re-equipped with the Mustang which, when carrying two drop tanks, could fly anywhere the bombers went. The provision of continuous fighter escort had cut the bomber losses dramatically by the summer of 1944. US fighters ranging over occupied territory and the enemy homeland, gradually achieved air superiority, so that the Luftwaffe no longer posed a major threat. Between the autumn of 1943 and the summer of 1944 the German fighter force had been largely neutralized by superior tactics and forces, with its aircraft having either been shot out of the sky or destroyed on their airfields by strafing. Only a few years before it had been thought that it was asking too much of any pilot in a fast single-engined fighter to fly for more than two hours, but by 1944 Mustang pilots were often in their cockpits for four or five hours and sometimes as much as seven. Even more creditable was the fact that they often operated in bad weather with only a radio homing call to bring them safely back to England.

Despite being confined to a small cockpit for long periods, a fighter pilot's mission did not involve the hours required of a bomber crew man. The fighter pilot rose later and, even if assigned to the penetration period of bomber escort,

Threshing wheat at Hawkes Hall Farm as a Havoc light bomber makes its approach to land at Wethersfield, March 1944.

take-off was not until after the bombers had been airborne for two or more hours. As endurance was so important, fighters took off from runways in twos and the three squadrons of a group would marshal on different runways so that the whole group could be got into the air as quickly as possible. The usual squadron formation consisted of 16 aircraft positioned in four flights of four, each flight flying slightly lower than the flight ahead so that the leaders could be easily seen and followed. A flight was staggered exactly like the finger tips of a hand and for that reason the formation was known as a "finger four". The flight was composed of two elements and an element consisted of leader and wingman. The wingman followed his element leader, his duty being to protect him from attack from the rear while the leader attacked the enemy. When leaving the vicinity of their airfield, the three squadrons of a fighter group were positioned with the lead squadron in the centre, higher and slightly ahead. Course would be set directly to the rendezvous point with the bombers to be supported, and altitude would be gained on the climb out across the North Sea.

If a fighter squadron returned to base still in its 16 plane formation the chances were it had seen no action with the enemy. If the flights or elements returned individually there had probably been a combat. The 8th Air Force fighter bases were situated in several eastern counties, from Essex to Norfolk and as far inland as Northamptonshire. Their locations had initially been decided by deployment on airfields without concrete runways or those not up to bomber standard.

Surprisingly, the chances of survival for a fighter pilot were no higher than for a bomber crew man. A major reason was the use of fighter aircraft in ground attack, particularly heavily defended installations such as enemy airfields. A single rifle bullet could cause a fighter to fall from the sky. The P-47 Thunderbolt used by 18 of the 21 9th Air Force fighter groups was by far the most durable of the three US fighter types in such an environment. Its air cooled radial engine could sustain battle damage yet still function whereas the liquid cooled engines of the Mustang and Lightning would quickly seize if the coolant was lost.

With the launching of the cross-Channel invasion on 6th June 1944, the 9th's fighters became generally committed to supporting ground forces, increasingly so by army units radioing for air attacks on enemy forces obstructing their advance. As soon as air strips had been constructed in Normandy, 9th Air Force P-47 units began to move from southern England and by October all 9th Air Force fighter, bomber and reconnaissance units had moved to the Continent. Only the troop carrier groups, equipped with Douglas C-47 Skytrains – known as Dakotas to the British – remained in England, and all but one of these transferred to bases in France during the early months of 1945. The duties of the troop carrier groups were, as their name implies, to carry military personnel and move supplies. There were more than 900 C-47s in 14 groups and they served to drop paratroopers for the D-Day landings and the Market-Garden (Arnhem) operation in September 1944 to secure bridges in the Low Countries.

Once the Allied armies had broken out from the Normandy bridgehead the C-47s were busy flying supplies from the UK to France. Troop carrier groups were deployed in three areas of England; south Lincolnshire, Wiltshire, and Somerset and Devon.

The 8th Air Force continued to operate from England, although two of its fighter groups were detached to fly from Continental bases at the time of the crisis caused by the Wehrmacht's Ardennes counter-offensive in December 1944. Peak strength for the heavy bomber groups reached 41 operating near to 3,000 Fortresses and Liberators. The latter, which had only been present in small numbers until the autumn of 1943, amounted to almost half the heavy bomber strength by the following June when the last bomber group became operational. However, five Liberator groups in Suffolk converted to Fortresses, the type equipping the rest of the groups in the 3rd Division. Great rivalry existed between those who flew the two different types of heavy bomber, with personnel tending to deprecate the other's aircraft. This reveals a measure of trust in the aircraft type flown, a view no doubt heightened by combatants who survived their operational tour. In truth there was little to choose between either type when it came to the chances of survival which, by the final months of hostilities, had improved to 78 per cent. With a decline in the loss rate, and a shortage of replacements, the heavy bomber tour had been raised from 25 to 30 missions and further, in the summer of 1944, to 35.

Medium bomber crews had originally been required to fly 40 missions, later increased to 60 when the targets were mainly against communications requiring only shallow penetration of enemy airspace. In fact the medium bomber force provided a crewman with a greater chance of surviving. Fighter and reconnaissance pilots were required to fly 300 combat hours for a tour which might mean 60-80 missions.

The 8th Air Force heavy bombers were diverted to attacking tactical targets in support of the cross-Channel invasion on many occasions during the spring and summer of 1944. When possible they resumed the strategic air war with the primary objective of destroying the

enemy's petroleum products industry. These attacks proved highly successful and gave some credence to the goal that strategic bombing had been set to achieve. Without fuel the enemy's aircraft could not take to the sky or his tanks advance. The shortage of fuel, resulting from successful Allied bombing, was soon evident.

While the heavy bombers could now go about their task with a high degree of protection from interception by enemy fighters, the anti-aircraft artillery fire became heavier, more concentrated and more accurate and was particularly so around the vital oil installations. A barrage of 100 or more bursting shells was a daunting prospect at many targets. Flak was, for the majority of airmen, far more foreboding than fighter attack. With flak, as one combatant put it, you just have to sit there and hope there isn't a shell with your name on it. Against fighters, most crewmen had a gun with which to hit back, reducing the feeling of helplessness. Anti-aircraft artillery never brought the high losses that concentrated fighter attacks did to the heavy bombers, although on occasions it claimed several bombers at one target. Flak continued to torment until the very last 8th Air Force mission of the war.

A look over the hedge: Marauders taxiing at Chipping Ongar, Essex, before take-off on a raid. Winter 1943-44.

During the months following D-Day, American escort fighters flying from England experienced little contact with enemy fighters. In such circumstances, following their assigned period of escort duty, they would descend to strafe – shoot-up ground targets – notably enemy aircraft on their airfields and rail traffic. Occasionally, strafing missions would be flown by fighters especially to destroy such targets. As this type of activity increased so did the defences encountered, particularly at Luftwaffe airfields, and in consequence the losses to fighters mounted. This did not deter, but a more judicious policy was introduced in the selection of targets and execution of attacks. By the final months of the war approximately 15 fighters were lost to ground fire to every one shot down by an enemy fighter.

The last US heavy bomber mission was flown from England on 25th April 1945. The strategic bombing campaign never achieved the goals its advocates had originally sought. Diversion of forces had delayed completion of 8th Air Force's full strength until the cross-Channel invasion was launched. Indeed, its heavy bombers did not really get into full stride to have a pronounced effect on German war industry until the final nine months of the war; even then it was frequently diverted to a tactical role in support of ground campaigns. However, the provision of

Another wartime dawn. Bomber formations etch the sky while a Mustang is made ready for its pilot.   (Robert Sand)

long-range fighter escort to protect the heavy bombers did provide an initially unplanned achievement, air superiority over occupied and enemy territory which was, in itself, a requisite to the success of a cross-Channel invasion. Moreover, the long-range fighters flying from England became an offensive force in their own right with their frequent harassment of enemy communications, particularly railways where the destruction was such that by 1945 most important rail traffic moved only by night to avoid the seemingly ever roaming fighters.

The cost to the 8th and 9th Air Forces flying from the United Kingdom was approximately 30,000 airmen killed or missing and a similar number made prisoner of war; over 6,000 heavy and 500 medium bombers missing in action and around 2,500 fighters. Even without enemy action flying in those days was a dangerous occupation. For every six aircraft lost on combat missions one was destroyed or crippled in accidents in Britain. The major cause can be attributed to human failures, either uncautioned flying by exuberant youth or some maintenance or repair failure. Additionally, design weaknesses would occasionally manifest themselves in aircraft which, after all, were viewed as expendable in the cause of bringing destruction to the enemy. Crashes became almost commonplace to the people of East Anglia where, on average, one aeroplane fell out of the sky every day. It seemed that each morning's gathering in the heavens brought some incident of death and destruction somewhere across the broad East Anglian plain, mostly transmitted as a muffled thump in the distance or a column of acrid black smoke on the horizon, but sometimes close at hand. Few villages escaped the mark of the air war.

We were the third ship to take off. We had just become airborne when the Fort nosed up and the left wing dropped. We seemed to be going around in a big curve and my first reaction was that our pilot was pulling a fancy manoeuvre. I got down on my left knee to look out the side window of the radio room in time to see the left wing throwing up dirt and sparks. Didn't have to be told we were in trouble and, expecting a crash, I turned to brace against the radio room door. As I did so it swung open and at first I thought someone was coming through. I held it and looked into the bomb bay but there was nothing to see except those 12 five hundred pounders. I shut the door and braced myself against it and realized the pilot had got us off the ground. The engines were groaning and I knew things were still very wrong. I glimpsed some guys standing by a hangar and wondered why I couldn't be there at this moment. The plane struck the ground again then cleared, but it was plain we weren't going to make it. I gripped the beading round the edge of the open radio room gun hatch and thought of trying to jump out but things were going past too fast. Then we hit the ground hard, tail first, and I found myself looking out where the tail had been. Pieces of fuselage were flying off and bulkheads moving around and the ball turret was crushed up inside. The wreck was slowing but I kept thinking about those bombs just the other side of that plywood door. A final big lurch and we came to a stop. I could see the reflection of flames on the aluminium skin. I heard Musser say let's get the hell out of here as he jumped up and stepped over Cohen who was lying by the ball turret. I walked over him too and out the fuselage side entrance. Cohen followed and we all went round to the front of the wing and saw the plane had hit a barn. The pilot had clambered out. He had blood running down his face. I was going back to get the bombardier and navigator but the pilot said they were dead and that we should get clear before the bomb load went up. We ran down the field towards the village. A man stuck his head out of the first house and said, "Did you hear a bang?" I said, "You gonna hear another one in a minute." We told him to get his family out and down the road. There was a straw stack in the field near the road and we all got behind that. People were now coming down the road like a load of refugees. I took a look back at the plane and saw it was burning fiercely. There was nothing the crash wagon could do but let it burn and get people away from neighbouring houses. Then, about 15 minutes later, there was one hell of a boom and for a moment the clouds in the sky turned red. Pieces started to fall, the heavy bits first and then the lighter pieces it seemed took a few minutes to come down. Many of the houses in the village were wrecked by the blast but no one was seriously injured. The bombardier and navigator survived too, so all the crew escaped with their lives, if not injury.
Robert V. Kerr

5 MAKING FRIENDS

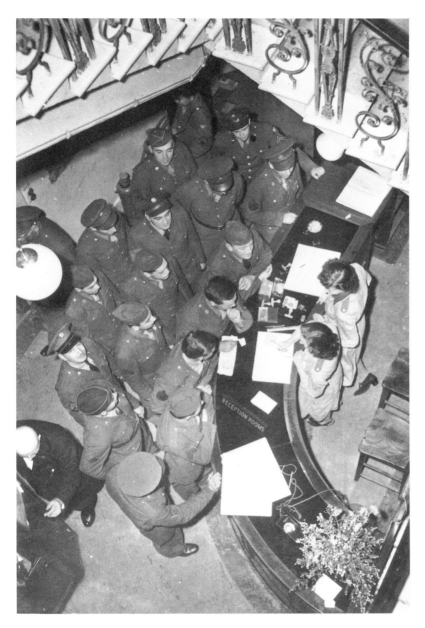

"Gotta room, Babe?" The reception desk at a London Red Cross Club in a requisitioned private hotel. The receptionists were British women employed by the American Red Cross organisation.

NOT ONLY did USAAF ground personnel outnumber aircrew 20 to 1, they had more contact with the British population. Operational air crew, leading a more restrained life, were usually too tired to venture much from base when off duty. Moreover, their stay in the UK was usually short, particularly towards the end of hostilities when many completed an operational tour in three months. Ground

men were normally with their assigned units for "the duration" and thus most with the 8th Air Force and many with the 9th were in the UK for at least a year. The number of men permitted to be off base at any one time was supposedly 15 per cent but USAAF establishments had fairly easy regimes.

Although an official pass was required to leave the camp, the widely dispersed living sites at bases, particularly airfields, made it easy for men to escape into the countryside. Providing a man was "off duty" a liberal attitude prevailed as to what he did or where he went. Officially or otherwise, GIs were at liberty to make bicycle explorations of the surrounding countryside in the evenings. With a pass the evening Liberty Run to the local town or city would be taken. It was often a Liberty Run convoy of a half dozen "6 x 6" trucks or British ex-civilian buses, with a 1900 hours departure and 2300 hours return. Apart from the pubs and cinemas, and on some nights dance halls, some large towns had a Red Cross Club. These were set up and administered by the American Red Cross organisation using a requisitioned hotel or large house. Amenities included a cafeteria, games room, lounges where the latest periodicals could be read and letter writing facilities. The scope, of course, depended on the space available and the size of the venue but all were well patronised by the local USAAF community. There were also Anglo-American Clubs sponsored by the Anglo-American Hospitality Committees of local people to promote and foster goodwill. The amenities were not so extensive as in the Red Cross Clubs but they were excellent places for gaining introductions to British families.

Leave periods depended on the discretion and requirements of unit commanders; enlisted men (the "other ranks" to the British) usually being able to obtain a 48 hour pass once a month. Officers had more flexible arrangements while combat crew airmen were often allowed two or three day passes during periods when the unit was "stood down". The favourite destination was London and there were few long-stay GIs that did not visit the capital city. Apart from the historic and entertainment attractions there were, eventually, 15 Red Cross Clubs in central London alone. Seven were strictly for enlisted men, four for officers and one, at 10 Charles Street, purely for women officers. The others catered for both officers and men, the most famous and largest being Rainbow Corner in Shaftesbury Avenue. Rainbow Corner, opened in December 1942, could host 2,000 men at a time and had a staff of over 400, the majority British, with American Red Cross employees holding administrative positions. This was also the usual form of staffing at the Red Cross Clubs in metropolitan areas. Large military bases also had American Red Cross facilities. Every major airfield had an Aero Club staffed by three American Red Cross girls with some help from local women.

Many of those who worked at Red Cross Clubs were volunteers, in London several being women of some prominence. For Al Zimmerman of 493rd Bomb Group, the dominant feature of his first visit to Rainbow Corner was one such personality:

> "At Rainbow Corner there was this lovely lady in an American Red Cross uniform who sat at a desk in one of the rooms. A sign on the desk read, 'Have Adéle Astaire write a letter home for you.' Adéle Astaire was the sister of Fred Astaire, the famous movie tap-dancer. She was also Lady Cavendish, having married into British nobility. I was one of the fascinated guys who went over to ask her to write a letter home for me, but I really did it so I could stare at her; I think she had the most gorgeous set of legs I've ever seen in my life."

The entertainment world established the Stage Door Canteen at 201 Piccadilly, early in 1944, another cafeteria type club with the attraction that celebrities of stage and screen were often on hand to entertain and actually do a little waiting at table. This establishment, however, was open to all allied service personnel. One former mechanic declares the only thing that he remembers about England was being brought coffee by Bob Hope at the Stage Door Canteen.

In London the US servicemen entered West End establishments that their British counterparts would shun because they were the places for the wealthy and privileged. It was not just a case of having more money in the pocket; rather the general American lack of class consciousness. Enlisted men dining on the next table to senior officers in exclusive hotels were not an unusual sight. There was nothing daunting in assailing the haunts of the aristocracy and titled. An insight into this is given by the experience and comments of a 386th Bomb Group bombardier, Edward Laube:

> "During a trip to London we went into a hotel named Grosvenor House which at the time was owned by Lord and Lady Townsend. Because of the black-out it was necessary to carry a flashlight which the British called a 'torch'. This rather elegant lady, who was Lady Townsend, admired the American flashlight which I promptly gave to her as a gift. She then took me to the desk clerk and advised that any time I wanted a room the hotel would accommodate me. Thereafter, any time I came to London I would bring her lemons and oranges which the British hadn't seen for years.
>
> As a result of this meeting she would invite me and some of my friends to her Sunday afternoon tea dances which featured the fashionable young women from some of the more classy families. I also became her favorite in that I would stand in the receiving line with her to greet Allied officers. Being located only fifty miles from London, the trip to town was only about one hour, so . . my social life improved with the addition of the Sunday dance. It tickled me to greet Generals and other high

The Bull Hotel was taken over as the principal Red Cross leave hostel in Cambridge – which, with seven other clubs, had the largest ARC group in the UK outside London. (Cal Sloan)

Rainbow Corner,
1945. (Cal Sloan)

ranking officers with me being a first Lieutenant. Because of the relationship I was always seated at her Ladyship's table. One of my friends, Lilburn 'Buck' Rogers, met his wife through the Sunday tea dance. I think that Lady Townsend was amused by me and my friends and I also served as a buffer.

In the three years since I left Chicago, the association with educated people and the new social contacts with sophisticated people left its mark on me. The air force uniform was a pass into anywhere. In the pre-war years I would have never ventured into some of the places that I now was at ease in. In short, they would never get me back on the farm after I'd seen Paree."

In spite of those general misgivings about "the bloody Yanks" those who made their acquaintance came quickly to like them. Lady Townsend, like another titled lady, probably found them "a breath of fresh air into our drab wartime existence".

The Anglo-American Clubs co-operated with the American Red Cross in introducing many thousands of US servicemen to British families who were prepared to welcome them into their homes. Not all visits were expected to be successful; often the two parties being too far removed socially or one or other having entered into the arrangement for the wrong reasons. A considerable number were not only successful but the bond of friendship established then was to

endure for a lifetime. A particular effort was made to encourage English families to offer the hospitality of their homes at Christmas when it was felt the GI would feel separation from "his folks" the most. Saul Kupferman, serving with the 306th Bomb Group at Thurleigh, was involved in one of the successes:

"At Christmas, 1943, British people near our base invited individual GIs to go along to their homes for the day. A Donald Nicoll went all out and accepted two of us (myself and Kenny Norris, a member of my crew) to share the holiday with his family. Don and his wife Dorothy were in their forties and they had a little six-year old daughter Cynthia. We knew all about how the English folks were rationed and the shortages so we were prepared to go easy on eating and drinking. They couldn't have done more to make us feel at home. I took along a box of chocolates which was obviously a special treat. They made it last for several days; rationing themselves to one each per day. I don't think 'Cindy' had ever seen chocolates before. After dinner I played darts with the father, who was a prison guard. On that first visit I remember the Morrison table shelter in the dining room and the threadbare towels which they couldn't replace because of the rationing. This was the start of a lifetime friendship and during the rest of my time in England I accepted the Nicoll's invitation to use their spare bedroom whenever I had passes. It was an escape from the military life and the home life atmosphere they provided I feel

33

sure helped me to survive. I recall making one mistake, and that took place on 4th July 1944. I went out in their backyard and shot off my .45 pistol into the air to celebrate. That sure upset Don Nicoll because he was the neighborhood warden!"

It was not just the deprivations of wartime that the visitors were seeing. The low wages and salaries were reflected in the poorer domestic standards than would have been found in the homes of Americans with equivalent jobs. GIs were usually observant enough to be aware they were in low income homes and responded by taking presents, usually foodstuffs, that would be very welcome. This was an open generosity, a true appreciation of kindnesses shown to them.

Rural homes of the time were even humbler but the occupants were, by all accounts, the most open-handed with hospitality towards the GIs. This was certainly the experience of Lt George Collar, a bombardier of 445th Bomb Group, while undergoing a theatre indoctrination course:

"Clontoe was on the banks of Loch Neagh, the largest lake in Ireland. One evening, a fellow by the name of Olson, from Long Island, was fooling around and fell in the lake. He was fished out by an eel fisherman named Peter Coyle. Coyle was a bachelor who lived with his parents and a married sister and her husband and their four children, aged about 3 to 12 years. They lived in an old stone cottage, with thatched roof, which had been in the possession of the family for over 250 years. Olson was taken to the house to dry out and warm up. As a token of his gratitude, Olson decided to visit them one evening, so he invited me along. We took our tobacco ration and some candy for the youngsters. We were treated like long lost relatives. They didn't have much, but they cooked eggs and toast and made a pot of tea. The tea kettle hung over a raised stone hearth, which contained a peat fire. After tea the children all lined up and sang Irish songs for us. Soon the whole family joined in. They could sing like larks. Before the evening was over we all sang. Olson was especially good as he had sung in light opera before the war.

After we bade the family goodbye, Peter Coyle took Olson and me to a large barn a couple of miles away where a group of travelling players were staging a play for the benefit of a large rural audience. Between the acts the Master of Ceremonies enter-

tained the audience by singing songs in rhyme about various people in the crowd. Before we knew it, he was singing about Olson and me. It came as a complete surprise and we were both flattered to say the least."

For the most part it was the enlisted men who took advantage of the Anglo-American Clubs or Red Cross arranged home visits. Ground officers mostly made their own contacts and they were also the chief recipients of overtures from the class-conscious middle and upper classes

British charity organisations provided refreshments for US servicemen at many of their bases. These mechanics at Shipdham "take tea" from a Church Army mobile canteen.

A party of WACs from the first contingent to arrive in Britain enjoy tea with Mrs Mary Wenger in the beautiful grounds of Aston Hall near Stone, Staffordshire.

The hand of royalty extended in friendship. King George VI arriving at Huntingdon railway station on 14 November 1942, for his first visit to USAAF airfields in England. Top Brass greeting him are Major General Carl Spaatz, commanding 8th Air Force; Major General Ira Eaker, commanding VIII Bomber Command and Brigadier General Newton Longfellow, commanding 1st Bomb Wing.

In flying kit, Major Lloyd Mason, a Fortress squadron commander, shakes hands with Princess Elizabeth during a royal visit to Kimbolton in July 1944. General Jimmy Doolittle, commander of 8th Air Force, looks on.

was a real honour. At noon he got his umbrella and bowler hat and we were off to his club located on the top floor of a three-storey building. He escorted me into the club and all of a sudden all eyes were on me and all activity ceased. He made a blanket introduction and the activities returned to normal. There was a pool game going on and I was invited to participate. I explained I was not much of a pool player but they eagerly persisted. I was assigned a partner who I'm sure was the best player in their club and, of course, we won. I could tell that they wanted to talk about the war and how it was going from our view but they were too polite to approach the subject directly. I tried tactfully to give them as much information as I could and they seemed very pleased with what I said. We had a nice lunch and after about two hours returned to the insurance office. Marjorie told me afterwards that I had made a good impression and that I had been accorded quite an honour by her boss. With the class system being what it was in those days I'm sure that had I not been an officer I probably would never have received that invitation."

One section of the British community that the GI had no difficulty in making friends with was the children. The bond was not just material as one might think from the legendary cry of "got any gum chum". Whereas a British young man who considered himself adult distanced himself from juniors to affirm his recently attained status, the American placed no such barrier. There was no stigma in associating with youngsters or taking a condescending attitude towards them. British tongue-in-cheek sarcasm held that the popularity of children with Americans was not surprising as the latter had never really grown up. Yet what was done for their children in wartime was really appreciated.

Children's parties were periodically held on most USAAF bases, where the hosts enjoyed themselves as much as their young guests. Undoubtedly the candy (sweets), chewing gum, chocolate bars, ice cream, oranges and other rare or unobtainable items that delighted young palates were a major attraction, but children also sensed they were not being patronised. Admittedly, these parties were encouraged by the US authorities who saw them as good public relations exercises. Further appealing to their men's soft spot for youngsters, a War Orphans Fund was set up under the auspices of the US

of British society. An officer indicated a certain standard of conduct and behaviour in British eyes as Lt Al Jones discovered:

"I used to date the sister of one of the Red Cross girls. She worked as a secretary for an insurance broker in Norwich. I would usually come by about noon when I was in Norwich and find out if we had a date for the current production at the Theatre Royal. On this particular occasion her boss came out of his office and asked if I would like to go with him to his club for lunch. I accepted with pleasure realizing that this servicemen's newspaper, *Stars and Stripes*, the object being to provide additional financial aid for British children who had lost one or both parents from war action.

Many English boys were attracted to aircraft and in loitering around airfield boundaries were befriended by ground crew men. Some youngsters even became mascots, fitted out with items of GI clothing. Others would willingly fetch and carry for their soldier friends. One lad at Mendlesham airfield had a regular out-of-school task of sweeping out the interior of his mechanic friend's bomber when it returned from operations.

The Americans' unbridled sentimentality probably played a part in the affection bestowed on children. It certainly did with the canine population, substantial numbers of which transferred home to USAAF bases. Acquisitions from pet shops accounted for a good proportion of these, although several strays magically found themselves the beneficiaries of American dog love. At certain airfields the matter got completely out of hand and by 1945 there were estimates of 50-150 in residence through airmen having passed on their companions after completing tours and returning to the States. It is said that firm action was ordered after General Partridge, commander of the 3rd Division, was incensed by a score or more dogs that insisted on joining a parade he was inspecting, particularly when two started

copulating. Dogs were not the only creatures that became GI pets. Cats, rabbits and British wildlife were supplemented by more exotic creatures such as snakes, monkeys, parrots and the like smuggled in from overseas. Despite the UK's strict quarantine laws, donkeys acquired in North Africa were to be found at Thorpe Abbotts and Snetterton Heath in Norfolk while at Framlingham in Suffolk a squadron of the 390th Bomb Group had a brown bear cub that flew with them from the US.

Brigadier General C.C. Chauncey hands out presents at Camp Griffiss, Busy Park children's party; 16 December 1943.

Several USAAF bases adopted war orphans in furtherance of the War Orphans Fund started by the servicemen's newspaper *Stars and Stripes* in September 1942. This is Yvonne, whose father was killed in the Royal Navy while serving at Portsmouth, being entertained by men of the 384th Bomb Group at Grafton Underwood.

'Roscoe Ann', the Framlingham bear cub. When this animal grew to maturity and frightened several of the farming folk in the vicinity of the base by its forays into their property, a quiet word from the local law resulted in the bear being put down.

Right: Sgt Anderson looks pleased with the chicks he reared at Deenethorpe. One suspects these were not really pets but ultimately intended to fulfil culinary objectives. (via Vic Maslen)

Far right: 'Lady Moe' of Snetterton Heath enjoyed eating cigarettes rather than smoking them.

This assortment of pets was resident at Boxted in August 1943. Left to right: Private Walter Kelly with 'Flak', T/Sgt M.E. Shank with 'Salvo', Private F. Carpole with 'Rose Bud' and S/Sgt James Marcus with 'Windy'. There was another pet duck but this disappeared, victim of a hungry GI.

Cavorting along the perimeter track at Framlingham, both 'Scrappy' the puppy and 'Joe' the monkey were flown into Britain from the US.

Christmas away from home is never pleasant, not even in Jolly Old England. With activities at the Stone Distribution Center shut down, Jim Tyson and I walked 4 miles into the town of Stone for want of something better to do. As we were walking down an avenue lined with yew trees, heading for a church, a middle-aged woman and a boy crossed the street and approached us. The woman spoke first saying, "Won't you Yanks come home and have Christmas tea with our family?"

Although somewhat startled by the gracious offer, Jim and I were quick to accept. We learned that the lady's name was Doris Redman and her companion was her 14 year old nephew, Paul Redman.

The Redman family home was part of a long row of homes built into one brick building that covered an entire block. I would say the family was probably middle or upper middle class by social standards. The house was full of people. Mr and Mrs Redman, the parents of Doris, were the hosts. He was a retired, or semi-retired manager of a local pottery, and much of the conversation was about this local industry for which this town in Staffordshire is famous. Paul Redman, the 14 year old boy and his 15 year old sister talked with youthful exuberance and enthusiasm about the "famous potters" who had lived in their community. Somehow, I couldn't associate glamour with the word "potter"; but the youngsters were undaunted.

One member of the family was an army Captain, home on leave from Montgomery's Africa Corps. He had been gravely wounded in a tank battle and walked with a severe limp with a cane to assist. But he seemed to be having a ball, and enjoying the gathering more than anyone, with the possible exception of Jim and I. We wondered where to find the "cold" and "aloof" English people we had heard so much about. They certainly weren't part of this group. Conversation flowed freely. The tea and scones were delicious; and we were treated with a warmth and friendship we hadn't seen since leaving home.

Reluctantly we gave our thanks, said goodbyes, and started to make our departure. However, Paul and his sister invited us to return the next day for a sightseeing tour of Stone if our duties permitted.

December 26, 1943. After a brief morning session we found we were free for the rest of the day. Jim and I walked the 4 miles into Stone and met with Paul Redman and his sister. "What shall we do?" I asked.

Paul Redman enthusiastically replied, "Oh, let's go for a walk."

After hiking more than 12 miles in two days, I really wasn't that excited. Nevertheless we saw every pottery in and around Stone and were treated to a fine historical review of every famous "potter" who had ever plied his trade in the vicinity, including one of my favorites, Josiah Wedgwood. But my dogs were really barking when Jim and I were ready to return to camp. Fortunately we were able to catch a ride on a GI truck, and we both survived a memorable afternoon.

John Howland

The devoutly religious took the opportunity to attend services in British churches and chapels. These are airmen from Snetterton Heath talking to the vicar of Quidenham, himself a military veteran of the First World War.

Stationed at Attlebridge in East Anglia, I was frequently on my bicycle whenever we had a standdown. How rich was that part of England, with each village offering history and literature of centuries past! A former student and teacher, I grasped every opportunity to get off base and satisfy curiosity. One day my CO, Colonel Pierce, told me he had seen a sign on a house that identified it as the Chaucer House, in the village of Bawdeswell. With everything under control in the operations center, I biked out that evening and found the owners of the house in their back garden. Mr and Mrs Lloyd Lewis welcomed me into their 14th century home, which had purportedly belonged to Chaucer's uncle. That evening marked the beginning of a wonderful friendship which was to last for 40 years. Both Lloyd and Adeline Lewis were gentle, well-educated people – he an engineer, and she village schoolmistress. They opened their home to me and my friends, a place where we could enter the quiet of that medieval village and their clay-and-wattle house, to have a cup of tea and hours of good conversation, a time and place where we could pretend for a while that there was no war that demanded our attention and efforts. I was introduced to people in surrounding homes and halls that I would not have known except through Mr and Mrs Lewis. Lloyd Lewis died in '51 and Adeline came to our California home for her first American visit. Later, she spent another winter with us. We maintained a correspondence for 40 years, our fine friendship enhanced by each well-crafted letter. My memories of that period of war in the ETO will forever be warm.
Henry Bamman

In January 1945 members of our crew were sent to rest homes for a week, the four officers going to Eynsham Hall near Oxford. On Sunday the Yanks at the Hall were transported to various places of worship and the party I joined went to a small Methodist church in the town of Witney. We were ushered to seats on the left side of the sanctuary as one faced the chancel. There was a balcony along the full length of the opposite side and in the end closest to the chancel was a group of children who had remained following Sunday School for the church service. The text of the sermon was introduced by the pastor's listing several leave-taking expressions, including "adios", "au revoir", the British expression of the day, "God bless", and what he thought was the predominant American expression, "so long". He then asked the children in the balcony which expression they thought was the nicest and most meaningful. Obviously he expected their reply to be "God bless" which would lead him nicely into his sermon. Those kids looked down at the dozen or so Yanks in their proper dress uniforms and shouted as one, "so long". Whether it was the novelty of having Yanks in the congregation or just that natural rapport that seemed to exist between the US servicemen and the British kids didn't matter, but those kids really made the day for some homesick young Yanks. We almost stood up and saluted our young friends. Needless to say, it took some adroit manoeuvring on the part of the pastor to get back on track with his sermon.
John Ramsey

With four American airfields in my district I had to liaise with their military police on all sorts of matters and I got to know some men very well. One character was a senior MP sergeant in charge of supplies for the local MP company. He was a former New York cop, of Italian background, and although he was a very good policeman he had a taste for the good things in life.

One evening I found an argument going on between some village men and this MP sergeant with a corporal who was with him in the patrol Jeep that conducted regular trips round the district. When I appeared the civilians left but I quickly saw that the two American MPs had been drinking. I told them to follow me down to my house where I got my wife to make some coffee to sober them up. This sergeant started to heap sugar into his cup until my wife quickly told him that what was in the bowl was our ration for the whole week. Anyway, the two men finally left but must have appreciated what we had done for them.

About 3 am I'm woken by a banging on my door. Looking out of the bedroom window there is the sergeant. I thought you and your wife would like this he said, indicating something he'd been carrying. It was a 10 stone sack of sugar! He seemed hurt when I told him to clear off. He added that he'd got some tinned fruit in the Jeep too. Well, I told him he'd be getting us both locked up. Finally he gets the message and goes. However, next morning when my wife opens the front door she finds the bag of sugar leaning against it. Now this really puts me in a spot because I can't take it back to the camp without making trouble for the sergeant, any more than I can keep it myself. So the sugar was very quickly given away to others in the village.

These fellows were embarrassingly kind. Whenever I drove up to the guardhouse I'd find some little present on the seat when I returned, usually stuff they'd bought in the PX store. One day the sergeant said to me, "I've put a little parcel in your car for your wife." It was small and light and I thought it must be silk or nylon stockings which they sometimes had in the PX. When my wife opened it there was a gross of condoms! She was a churchwoman, straight as a gun barrel, and she was really upset. "Don't you ever bring that dreadful man here again", she threatened. The sergeant probably meant it as a joke, but he picked the wrong person there.

The same sergeant got to know a woman in a nearby village and became a regular visitor. He used to drive there in a Jeep but the MP officer got to hear about this and stopped him using it. The sergeant then got the regular nightly Jeep patrol to drop him off at the woman's house and pick him up a few hours later. The trouble was that they were often different drivers who didn't know which house to call at. To find him they drove up and down the village street sounding the hooter. This brought complaints and I had to tell the sergeant to do something about it. The drivers stopped hooting but started knocking on doors to find the sergeant, which brought more complaints. The MP captain then banned his people from taking the sergeant to call on the woman but somehow he kept up his visits.

One Friday morning when I visited the Guard House, the sergeant and one of his friends were all dressed up in their best uniforms. I asked where they were going and was told Glasgow. They had a three day pass, plenty to spend and they'd heard that Glasgow girls liked Yanks. I warned him that the sort of Scots girls he was looking for would probably rob him. He just laughed and said he could look after himself all right. Sunday morning I went into the Guard House and there's the sergeant and his friend. I asked why they were back so soon. They had taken a couple of girls into a Glasgow hotel on Friday evening and had all their money stolen.

On another occasion when I went into the Guard House it was pretty clear that this sergeant was in a flaming bad temper. When he was out of the way I asked one of the clerks what was the matter. He said that the previous night someone on the base had given the sergeant a skinned rabbit ready for the pot. He had cooked and eaten it in his room but this morning he had been told it was not a rabbit but a cat that had been run over.
Jack Neasham

Unwanted long grass on airfields was a source of hay for local farmers, but the hay could be a fire hazard. Men of 325th Service Group at Chelveston load a truck in July 1943.

6 INN-HOUSE ENTERTAINMENT

WITHOUT doubt the most famous British institution as far as the GI was concerned was the pub, for there was nothing that truly corresponded to this in the USA. On arrival in the UK servicemen were advised by the military authorities that the public house or inn was as much for social intercourse as for drinking and that most pubs had their "regulars" who met to enjoy the company of friends "over a pint". Pubs were a natural starting point for any Yank who wanted to meet Limeys and to learn about the people and the country. There were a lot of pubs, particularly in East Anglia where towns like Ipswich and Bury St Edmunds seemed to have at least one pub in every street. Much like the natives, individual GIs settled on one or two particular pubs, usually after learning that there were those that only catered for working class trade, some for the well-to-do (although they usually advertised themselves as hotels), while most catered for class and pocket by a public bar and a saloon, the latter having higher charges for purchases. There were also additional rooms in many houses with

such curious names as Snug, Tap Room, Pot Room and others.

For those unbriefed, British beer was often a disappointment as it was not the lager type beer popular in the States. In the first place it was rather flat and, secondly, it was not chilled. Cold drinks were available in certain hotels in big cities but a refrigerator was a rare facility in the average pub. There was some variety: pale ale, bitter, brown stout and special beers such as Bass and Guinness, but all quite different from the beer in the bars back home. The GIs regularly complained about the warm, flat beer but many soon developed a taste for it. The alcohol strength was variable, even so, as many an unwary drinker discovered, it could have quite a kick. Getting drunk was no problem. Roger Armstrong, a radio operator in the 91st Bomb Group at Bassingbourn, recalls, "We were admonished to be temperate in our consumption of English beer. We were reminded that American beer was 3.2 per cent alcohol whereas the British beer was strong enough to make our tongues 'wag at both

A quiet pint with the landlord and his wife in a Bassingbourn pub. (Cal Sloan)

ends'. Since I was not much of a drinker the warm beer did not bother me. In fact, I acquired a taste for it." Earl Robinson, an armourer with 479th Fighter Group at Wattisham, also found the beer strange, but what really surprised him was when he saw some old men in a pub stick a poker in the fire and, when red hot, stick it in their pint of beer to make it even warmer!

The supply of beer was limited by the brewer who rationed each public house to a specified amount every week. The ration would have catered for the requirements of the regulars without reduction in their consumption. With Allied servicemen stationed in the vicinity of the pub, the ration did not endure for long. Some publicans endeavoured to restrict customers on a daily basis; most simply sold on demand and then put out "No Beer" signs until the next supply. It became a habit for some GIs to drain a pub and then move elsewhere, a tactic that made them very unpopular with the regulars. Particularly when the regulars were working late. At a Dedham farm the harvesters were always treated to a pint in the local pub after the day's work. One evening in August 1944 the harvesters arrived for their well deserved sustenance to be met outside by Willie Frost, one of their band who had gone ahead of the rest. "Wha's the matter, Willie?" His anger was plain to see. "No Beer" he hissed. "No beer? That were only due in this afternoon. What's happened?" another harvester queried. "Why, the bloody Yanks of course. They've bin here early and drunk the place dry." Willie lived to be 80 but he never had a good word for Uncle Sam after that evening. A countryman will forgive most misdemeanours, but he who deprives him of his beer is an enemy for life.

Another irritation was the deeper pocket of the GI who could afford liberal amounts of ale. By 1944 a pint of bitter was 10 pence (16 cents) which was expensive for a farm worker whose standard wage was the equivalent of 50 pints. However, the average GI was generous and regularly treated those acquaintances in his adopted pub. Hard liquor was more difficult to find and what few bottles a publican could acquire were kept "under the counter" for favoured customers. Many Americans were in this category although at 25 shillings a bottle (5 dollars) it was expensive even to them.

The pub was a place for talking and also introduced the GI to the table games of Shove Ha'penny and Cribbage as well as the dartboard on the wall. Lt Robert Coffin was introduced to darts during off-duty pub visits: "I soon found I was pretty good at it. Guess it didn't go down too well with the old English guys in the *Three Cocks* at Brigstock as they tried to make out that when I threw a dart it might go anywhere. As soon as I walked in the pub door they would shout, 'Grab your tin hat and take cover, that Yank's here'."

Another feature of the pub was musical entertainment, singing round a piano, and GIs would often join in. WAC Elenor Frederick's observation was that in the pubs you often saw a British boy sit down and play the piano, as most pubs had one in the saloon. At that time it would have been most unusual to see an American serviceman do this as he would have been looked upon as being a cissy.

Many country pubs and those in the poorer town districts were very basic establishments, while those at the other end of the market provided considerable comfort and good amenities. Lt Jack Bryant recalls how very basic was the first pub he visited near his Sudbury base. "After partaking of various beverages over the course of the evening it was necessary to make use of a facility euphemistically called a "water closet". A closet it certainly was not. It was outside in the back of the building and consisted of a partially

Every pub had a dartboard and some US servicemen were so taken with the game they acquired a board on which to practise the art in the base "club". Second Lieutenant Edward Hennesay, of 303rd Bomb Group is seen here retrieving his darts.

A summer evening's relaxation at Catworth *Fox*, Huntingdonshire, on the A604 road. (Quenton Bland)

Below: A jolly time at Debden. Base bars were preferred by many men and civilian friends could be entertained by invitation. The beer was still of British origin. (N. Lippman)

enclosed slate wall with a diagonal trough at the base. There was no lighting because of blackout requirements and overcast clouds limited any natural light. It was not quite pitch black, but it was close to it. Two or three local customers were occupying the available space, facing the wall, while I waited my turn. Then one of the Englishmen spoke to another beside him, showing a forbearance impossible for an American. What he said was, 'Pardon me old chap but you're urinating on my leg'."

The GI took readily to the wartime pastime of autographing walls and ceilings. Where they were allowed British servicemen left their signature on pubs they had visited, a practice which spread to their ally, but was very much dependent on the goodwill of the landlord. Most of this graffiti was removed in post-war years as being unsightly. In a few places it was seen in a different light and has been preserved, notably at *The Swan*, Lavenham and *The Eagle* in Cambridge. Some famous names are among those left by American customers during the war years.

Saturday March 11, 1944

Another easy day for us. Flew about three and a half hours on a practice flight. In the evening Bill Doherty and I rode our bikes to *The White Hart* in Great Yeldham and had a few drinks and dinner. This is a very old inn on the stage road between Colchester and Cambridge. The huge oaken doorsill is deeply worn by the many thousands of feet that have crossed it; so deeply in fact that a half-moon shaped board has been fitted to the bottom of the heavy door to fill a gap approximately four inches deep. The atmosphere is typically English. Windsor backed chairs seem almost too delicate for the commercial service they are subjected to in the dining room, and the huge open hearth and lounge chair comfort of the adjoining pub room provides a home-like atmosphere.

Shortly after our arrival at Ridgewell I was having a pint of mild in the pub room when I had the opportunity to watch a sergeant gunner from the base perform his classic act. The young American from the New York city area could speak with an absolutely perfect cockney accent and the middle aged owner of the inn seemed to love him like her son. Occasionally, a British salesman or traveller would stay overnight at *The White Hart* and the sergeant would strike up conversation using his realistic cockney accent. Invariably his pigeon would ask, "What are you doing wearing an American uniform and flying with the Yanks? Why aren't you in the RAF?" "Oh, I *was* in the RAF," replied the sergeant. "But the bloody conditions were impossible. The food was bad, the uniforms were scratchy and the pay awful. So I joined up with the Yanks." Then, without explaining how he had accomplished such a miracle, he would rejoin his comrades, who also played the game. Everyone kept a straight face and didn't break into peals of laughter until the pigeon left the room.

The atmosphere had changed the evening Bill and I went to dinner. We were not unwelcome; but the sergeant gunner was missing in action. The proprietress tearfully informed us she was terribly tired of war and it would be best for all concerned if we Yanks stayed on the base.

John Howland

We had just flown the north Atlantic route via Greenland and Iceland to Prestwick, Scotland. We got as far as Cheddington in the English midlands and it was our first stopover in the UK. This was near a small rural market town called Dunstable, as yet not too familiar with Americans, much less airmen.

The first place we went was a pub in the middle of the town. They had not seen many Americans before. A group of us, enlisted men and officers, crowded up to the bar. We had been there only a short time when somebody in the group suggested that we make a party and asked the bar keeper if she could tell us what the entire stock of liquor and beer in the pub was worth. Quite taken aback by this request the bar keeper went behind the bar and into the back office to talk to the owner. She came back in a matter of minutes with the owner in tow. The owner was as much surprised as she was and asked us why we had made this request. We said we had just that day arrived in merry old England from the United States and were heading for combat duty. We wanted to have a party and in order to do so we needed a goodly supply of hard spirits. The pub owner got out his pencil and paper and figured out that the liquor in the pub was worth so much. He handed the piece of paper to one of the officers who looked at it and immediately dug into his pockets and took off his hat and passed it round to the others in our group. We all put some of the English pounds we had obtained at Prestwick into the hat.

"That'll do it lads" said the pub owner as he counted out the money on the bar, adding that the place was theirs for the party. For the rest of that evening we had one huge party staying in the pub until closing time. I recall running to catch the tailboard of the last convoy truck out of town back to the base and just managed to grab it in the darkness of the blackout. We left the next day for our combat base at Shipdham and I never saw that town or pub again but I will always remember that party.

Forrest S. Clark

CONTACT and friendships quickly highlighted differences in tastes, customs and habits. Food and drink was a noticeable area; the British quickly learning that coffee and doughnuts, more correctly dough rings, were as big an obsession with the newcomers as tea was with them. American coffee was strong by British tastes, their own brew being considered no better than "muddy water" by the GIs. The coming of the Yanks gave people in the UK their introductions to chilli con carne, peanut butter, coke and other delights of the American palate. As far as can be gauged few natives became enthusiastic about their allies' tastes.

Eating with the fork in the right hand, yet transferring it to the left every time the knife was taken up, was an American habit which intrigued their hosts; it was so out of keeping with the commonsense behaviour that characterised US practice. Indeed more than one USAAF flyer, who had been shot down over enemy occupied territory and escaped capture, finally gave himself away by eating with a fork in the right hand. As for the content of the plate, the uninitiated Briton was surprised to see GIs add jam or tinned fruit to meat and vegetables; mixtures of sweet and savoury being a common choice. The strictures of food rationing in the UK were impressed on GIs by the USAAF authorities and when dining with British friends most Americans were considerate enough to take only frugal helpings. Gifts of foodstuffs were another feature of such visits. In any case, much British food was not to American tastes. Those who had experienced meals in British messes considered them atrocious or, at best, unappetizing – as, for that matter, did many British servicemen. Wartime food in the UK, whether civilian or military, was not popular; the opinion of Sgt Irving Shapiro of the 94th Bomb Group being typical:

> "The word was around the base that the British food was pretty bad. They put sawdust in their sausages because meat was in short supply. Tasted that way the first and only time I bought sausage and chips in a Bury St Edmunds restaurant."

Despite the general view there were exceptions. Captain Harley Stroven, of 486th Bomb Group at Sudbury, took to something which was not overly popular with the English themselves:

> "The bread would arrive at the mess site in GI trucks; the bare loaves unwrapped and lying like so much stove wood, open to the air. But it was good!
>
> I loved that English bread. In my Nissen hut I usually had a loaf. There its texture and flavour reached its peak when toasted over a coke fire, butter melting into its savoury goodness.
>
> The memory of this would be retained, and for years back in Michigan I would tell my family of my love affair with English bread.
>
> I think it was probably as late as the 1970s that I purchased and brought home on a whim a loaf of English muffin bread. It was a new item on our stores shelf. When I bit into that first piece of toast I knew I had found it again."

The standard of menus and cooks varied from mess to mess and even if prepared for Americans by fellow countrymen there could in time be a certain monotony. The tinned pork-based meat loaf Spam tended to feature too often, particularly on toast, where it became vilified as SOS, the OS standing for "on a slice". Fresh meat and vegetables, coming from British sources, led to mutton and brussels sprouts becoming the major aversions. Brussels sprouts, despite mass objections, continued to feature as a main hot dish vegetable throughout the winter months to become a bad joke. Colonel Stanley Wray, commander of the 91st Bomb Group at Bassingbourn and a delightful humorist, once completed a combat mission briefing session by advising his pilots that if they had to crash on return to England to do so in a brussels sprouts field.

Some GIs took to a major British refreshment that was not rationed to add variety to their diet. Sgt Roger Armstrong, another Bassingbourn airman:

"At times the men in my bay in the barracks tired of the combat mess hall food. A number of us would decide we wanted fish and chips. One of us would volunteer to ride his bike to Royston, the nearest town. The owner of the fish and chips house would wrap our orders in old newspapers as there was a shortage of wrapping paper and boxes. Fish and chips were the original 'fast food' services in Europe. The chips were more like a steak fried potato, fried in deep fat. The fish was a white fish that was boneless. It was fried in a batter and the two together were very good. On the road back to base I usually found I had a number of English people on bikes following me as I had a light on my bike. There was a shortage of batteries and they were expensive for the local people during the war. We carried our fish and chips in a gunny sack in which potatoes had been shipped from America to our base."

Powdered egg was another common abhorrence and only air crew, in pre-mission breakfast, were served fresh eggs from the limited quantity allocated to each combat station. As every farmer and many householders in the surrounding country-side kept chickens, off duty egg forays were popular and often rewarding. The base PX (Post Exchange) provided many commodities and articles rationed or scarce in British shops, and as every GI had an entitlement to specified amounts of confectionery, tobacco and toiletries, it was not difficult to find a local who was willing to exchange fresh eggs for such scarcities. Farm eggs were rationed but this did not stop surreptitious transactions. Eggs were not the only potential culinary acquisition in the countryside if one got to know the right people. A pal who was a cook or mess orderly could really enhance such trading and olive drab painted tins of peaches, peanut butter and other delicacies were to be found secreted in country pantries.

Foraging, as with any desirable activity or objective in the English countryside, demanded some form of transport. Strict petrol (gasolene) rationing restricted the mileage of those few British people who could still run a car (auto) on essential work and there was no ration for private motoring. Public transport was crowded and often did not pass close by a military camp. The British public cycled – biked –

and so did the GI if he wanted to get around. The USAAF obtained a limited number of cycles from the British for issue to those personnel who had some distance to travel to their duties on airfields. There were insufficient to meet all needs and the unlucky had to go out and purchase a civilian cycle if they wanted to be mobile. The bicycle was not a common form of adult transport in the USA and a good proportion of GIs had never before attempted to ride one. The high UK models with lever brakes were difficult to handle which, with a lack of road sense, brought many tumbles. It was claimed that

A busy PX (Post Exchange) at a London Red Cross establishment. (Imperial War Museum)

Sergeant Cal Sloan and the tandem cycle he purchased and used to tour parts of Britain in 1945. The photograph was taken at 1.40 pm on 6 June 1945 outside Fen Ditton church, Cambridgeshire. (Cal Sloan)

in the winter of 1942-43 most patients in the Diddington US hospital near Huntingdon had been injured in cycle accidents. It is apparently more difficult to master a cycle when coming to it for the first time as an adult, particularly if one is accustomed to taking refreshment as Stanley White recalls:

"With the extended daylight hours provided by Double British Summertime, airmen from the B-24 bomber base at Wendling, the home of the 392nd Bomb Group, took off on what came to be known as 'Low-Level Missions.' These occurred when there was no combat alert for the following day.

Scores of Wendling inhabitants mounted their trusty bicycles and headed for pubs in such villages as Castle Acre and Swaffham. A few pints consumed by the riders often had a definite effect on the GI's sense of balance. There were numerous casualties from these missions.

My buddy from Powell Station, Tennessee was mounted on a most unruly vehicle. After several spills, he picked up the bike, carried it down a hill, and tossed it into a stream. He then started on the five mile hike back to the base."

There was also the hazard of the "wrong

It was easy to forget you should ride on the left and not the right in those country lanes. Two members of the 44th Bomb Group out for a spin near Southburgh church, spring 1943. (William Cameron)

side of the road", typified by Ivan Brown's experience when he set out from Halesworth airfield:

"I was heading for The Dog pub one evening. Hadn't met any traffic so, not thinking, was riding my bike on the right-hand side of the road as if I was back in the States. Suddenly a lorry comes round a corner, head-on towards me. I dodged out of the way by pedalling off the road, finishing up in a bramble bush."

Many vehicle accidents were as a result of instinctively reverting to the right-hand side of the road. The winding nature of many English roads was also the downfall of GI drivers who discovered the hard way that there is often a very deep ditch bordering the metalled highway. A large number of drivers had been taught to drive on enlisting and had only limited experience before finding themselves having to drive heavy trucks in the UK. Youthful exuberance probably played its part in the all too common habit of driving too fast for safety along the winding narrow lanes.

A Hampshire farm worker on a tractor pulling a seed drill that took up the whole width of a country road was astonished to see a Jeep suddenly come hurtling round a corner towards him, turn abruptly off the road straight through a post and wire fence, drive along the adjoining field until it came to a gateway behind him and then drive out onto the road without even reducing speed. A number of US servicemen terminated their existence by colliding with other vehicles, brick walls, trees and buildings. The hasty driver of a 6 x 6 truck, confused by his first encounter with a roundabout on the A12 at Colchester, lost control and plummeted down a steep embankment to spread his camp's laundry all over the main London rail lines.

Finding one's way to a specified destination was far from easy as signposts had been removed at the time of the invasion threat in 1940; most were not replaced until near or after the end of hostilities. Matters were made worse in that the agricultural depression of the twenties and thirties had let many hedgerows grow wild and tall so that seeing far ahead on the winding lanes was often impossible with a consequential disorientation. In this situation a stranger could set off cycling and some time later find he was back where he

started. Asking the way might bring a helpful response from a local but was invariably confusing: "You can't get there from here" being one puzzler to the uninitiated GI. The fact that place names and directional signs were missing in England was not immediately obvious to new arrivals from the States. Personnel of the 100th Bomb Group, travelling by train to Diss, Norfolk (for security a destination unknown to all but a few senior officers) kept lifting the carriage blackout curtains at every stop, hoping to get a clue to their whereabouts. One man announced that they were just passing through Moy. At the next station the same individual took another look and announced; "This Moy must be one hell of a big place". What he was seeing was the hoarding sign of one of the largest coal merchants in East Anglia who had rail collection yards at most stations.

A definite profiteer from the American invasion was the taxi business, handicapped only by petrol rationing. The greatest fear of taxi drivers was damage to their vehicles for frequently a stop to pick up a fare would see the vehicle over-filled by a rush of GIs all wanting to get back to camp. Pleading restrictions on numbers carried usually fell on deaf ears and in the

blackout a driver was often not aware of exactly how many passengers were aboard until they left. A taxi driver in Bedford, having been assured that "there's only six of us aboard Pop" was amazed to see fourteen tumble out through the light of a torch shone by an apprehending policeman who had witnessed the mad scramble.

"Not enough petrol" was the taxi driver's best excuse to avoid being hassled, but often the truth. There was one way round fuel shortage as fighter pilot Lt Curtis Smart discovered:

"I had gone to a party in Cambridge and had left late. I was scheduled to fly the next morning and didn't dare miss a combat mission. I got into a taxi and told the driver to take me to Honington. I went to sleep and when the driver woke me and said we had arrived I found we were in Huntingdon! He'd misheard my southern accent. When I told the driver I had to get back to Honington because I had to fly a combat mission, he said he didn't have petrol to get that far – around 40 miles – and he had no coupons to get more. Well, I was not very happy about this. Anyway, he says that Military Officers on vital war business had the right to commandeer taxis in an emergency. Okay, I said, this is an emergency and you are commandeered. He found a garage

The English car is on its right side of the road on the left. The six by six truck is on its wrong side of the road on the right. The resulting crash occurred on a Northamptonshire highway in February 1944.
(via Quenton Bland)

that had petrol. I signed some kind of paper, and he got the petrol. Fortunately, he got me back to Honington and I flew the mission."

It would be unfair to suggest that many cab drivers were avaricious and over-charged, but there must have been sufficient so inclined for the reputation to have existed. A Royal Navy officer recalls two occasions when he was shunned by taxis in favour of US officer fares and feels this was either due to the expectation of good tips or the possibility of overcharging if his fares did not understand the currency, which was often the case. Daphne Chute, a British woman working for the Americans and wearing her US military uniform, had the experience of being asked a double fare by a taxi driver. Calvin Hill of the 364th Fighter Group was also in no doubt about greedy tendencies:

"On a 'forty-eight' in London, I left a party at around 11.30 pm to go back to my hotel. Found there was a real bad fog, couldn't see your hand in front of your face in the blackout. Asked a taxi driver to take me back to my hotel but he said with the dimmed lights he had he couldn't see which way to go. So I volunteered to lead the way until he could. Started off walking with one foot on the kerb and the other in the gutter. Ended up walking the whole two miles back to my hotel with this taxi following. When we got there the driver wants full fare and I never even got into his cab!"

Difficulties in understanding the denomination of British coins and equating values with US currency was soon recognized by the unscrupulous as a means of cheating US servicemen. It should be stressed that such people were a very small percentage of the population. Thousands of GIs who did not understand "this Mickey Mouse money" simply offered a handful to a shopkeeper, publican, bus conductor or the like, who took the exact coinage for the service and not a penny more. Bill Sullivan tells of one of the exceptions he encountered:

"Upon arriving at Prestwick, Scotland we turned over our new B-17, changed our money for British pounds and were bussed to Glasgow to await our train for our new base. There was a pub at the station where some of us went for a brew. Upon being served we were examining the coins in our change out of curiosity when an old lad seated at a nearby table came over to us.

He inquired as to what we had given the waitress. He then asked to see our change. When we showed him he said, "You've been done for thrupence lads."

Even the pronunciation was confusing: "Thrupence" was three pence, yet the small coin with three pence printed on it was called a "thrupenny bit". A half-penny was spoken of as a "ha-penny" while the sixpence, shilling and two shilling coins could be referred to as tanners, bobs, and florins respectively. The information that 12 pennies made a shilling and 20 shillings made a pound was all very well but when one had to do the mental arithmetic necessary to convert a sum to cents when there were four dollars to a pound, it could become very confusing to the newcomer.

Another feature of wartime Britain the GI found confusing was rationing. Everyday materials and commodities that were plentiful in the USA were unobtainable or in restricted supply. Although GIs were mindful of the situation it often seemed to them that rationing was used as an excuse by the shopkeepers, publicans and caterers who did not want to do business with Americans – which may have been the case where the seller felt he should keep his wares for his hard-pressed countrymen and not the bountiful invaders. A Framlingham shopkeeper recalled that through the two year period USAAF personnel were in the district he had continuing requests from the unaware for items that were rationed. Lt John Howland, a 381st Bomb Group navigator, during a visit to London recorded the following in his diary for 5th February 1944, which is applicable to this propensity:

Feb 5, 1944
..... I tried to buy a handkerchief since I seem to be coming down with a cold, and in my haste I forgot to put one in my pocket yesterday. However, ration coupons are needed to buy cloth goods, and I didn't have any coupons, so I couldn't get a handkerchief. A middle-aged lady was standing nearby while I was trying to buy the handkerchief. She wore a very attractive wool tweed suit. The cloth looked like it was at least a quarter of an inch thick and brand new. I spoke to her saying, "Lady, that beautiful tweed suit of yours must have cost you at least one year's worth of ration coupons." She laughed and replied, "oh no, I didn't spend a single coupon for it. I bought it eight years ago."

Clothes rationing was very severe and British eyes were soon turned towards some of the garments worn by their ally. For a civilian to wear US military apparel openly would have brought investigation by the police but many a farm worker with friends at a nearby airfield sported a GI shirt or fatigues (overalls) while toiling in the fields. Even the lightweight cotton caps were popular as they could be washed. But the most prized acquisition was a pair of GI shoes. These were lace-up boots to the British, their appeal being the rubber soles and heels at a time when the UK working man's boot was heavy leather with metal stud protection.

Coming from a land where the cities and towns were brightly lit after dark, the UK blackout took some getting used to, particularly on moonless and overcast nights when it was "pitch black". If fog, reinforced with chimney smoke, was added to the scene, finding one's way was exceedingly difficult. Cigarette glow could be the only light visible in a narrow back street, which led to the aphorism that it was easy to tell a Yank in the blackout because of his cigar glow.

The blackout, of course, was anathema to the cyclist, adding to the likelihood of the unaccomplished ending up in a road-side ditch. The screened lighting allowed on cycles and motor vehicles did little more than illuminate a small area on the ground a few yards ahead making safe progress astonishingly slow. Dimmed and screened lighting was also allowed to illuminate the entrances to air raid shelters and other important buildings. The meagre light in telephone kiosks did nothing to lessen the mysteries of the British telephone system for the average GI. Indeed, the "red booths" became an irritating joke among US personnel due to the combined complexities of their coinage operation which, even when the "Press Button A" and "Press Button B" procedure had been mastered, rarely seemed to establish a connection. It took surprised GIs time to realise that the operator's curt "you're through" did not mean their time was up.

The British civilian police were also something of a joke to many GIs who could not accept the fact of unarmed law men. Most did come to respect the British bobby and go more in apprehension of their own military police who did "tote a

gun". Every major town in the vicinity of large USAAF concentrations had a station detachment of Snowdrops, the appella-tive for MPs' white helmets, belts and spats. Any British who, through viewing too many Hollywood films, had the notion that the US was rife with gangsters, could be forgiven for assuming this to be true if encountering a USAAF payroll collection. The monthly journey of the base finance section men to obtain the currency from a humble English bank was escorted by MPs with hand guns or carbines at the ready. A farmer about to go into Barclays in Princes Street, Ipswich, found himself confronted with MPs with drawn guns and the request to "hold it Pop, just while our guys come out with the loot".

About to brave the peculiarities of Britain's GPO telephone system. Captain Richard Graves (L), a flight surgeon, and Lt Jay Brekkon, both members of 848th Bomb Squadron. (Arnold Delmonico)

One of the most prized souvenirs was a bobby's helmet, for which considerable sums of money were paid. Captain Allen Sherman, a B-26 Marauder pilot of 387th Bomb Group, shows off his trophy. (Karl Berry)

Below: This airman, who picked a snowball fight with a couple of Belfast girls, seems to have got the worst of the battle. (via Vic Maslen)

Most GIs assumed that a "citizen's right to carry arms" pertained in Britain as it did in the USA and did not know that civilian possession and use of firearms was strictly controlled. Similarly, a man accustomed to being able to hunt in wild country with little restriction saw no reason why he could not do the same in the UK. The almost casual attitude to guns displayed by American servicemen was of some concern to the British authorities, to say nothing of country folk who had experienced bullets whistling past them when their presence was unknown to men engaged in illicit hunting. Despite the use of weapons for other than military purposes being forbidden, with a stiff punishment if caught, many GIs, taking a chance, went hunting pheasants and rabbits with carbines and hand guns. On the other hand, farmers and landowners invited American friends to join organised shoots and their guests usually brought the 12-bore shotguns used for "skeet" (firing at clays).

Poaching – as the British considered it – was too great a temptation and resulted in a few nasty incidents, notably the murder of a former diplomat, Sir Eric Teichman. His body was found in undergrowth not far from his home at Honingham Hall, Norfolk on the morning of 4th December 1944. An investigation revealed that the previous afternoon, hearing prolonged discharge of guns in woodland, Sir Eric had confronted two GIs, one of whom shot him through the head with a .30 carbine, the standard weapon issued to ground men at nearby Attlebridge airfield. A private with eight previous Court Martials and prison sentences in the States was convicted of murder. Lady Teichman made unsuccessful appeals to General Eisenhower's headquarters and the US Ambassador for the convicted man's life to be spared but to no avail. He was hanged on VE Day, 1945.

When 2 million men stop or pass by, some crime is inevitable and other murders, rapes and assaults were committed against British people by US servicemen. The extent of these incidents was apparently no greater than with any military force in a friendly foreign land.

Perhaps the most notable "difference" for Americans serving in the UK was the weather. The general continental climate of the United States conditions the population to regular hot summers and cold winters in northern latitudes and variance in high temperatures for southern seasons. Only in the north-west coastal states is there some similarity to Britain's climate. Most men, particularly those from arid places like Arizona or New Mexico, had difficulty in adjusting to the cool, damp conditions often prevalent in the UK. Upon arrival, a large number of GIs quickly succumbed to respiratory infections and many were regularly plagued by colds, the climate being adjudged the main cause for their susceptibility. The GI gained the impression that it was always raining in England and wisecracks about the wet weather were common, the most well known being that the island was waterlogged and it was only the barrage balloons preventing the place from sinking. In reality, rainfall in the area of most USAAF bases is not excessive – 18-24 inches per annum. However, frequent weather fronts moving in from the Atlantic give a preponderance of cloud, sealing in the dampness during winter months. The limited sunshine and the damp that seemed to invade both person and property was a depressing factor for several US servicemen, often assuming such significance for the individual that the still plentiful fair weather days are overlooked in hindsight.

The first friends we made in Halesworth were a Mr and Mrs Tom Greenacre and son Kenneth. Mrs Greenacre operated a tiny candy shop on the main street, Mr Greenacre was employed at a local dairy, and their son was still at school. We enjoyed many pleasant evenings with them; sometimes at tea-time and sometimes sharing their evening meal in spite of the severe rationing in effect during the war years.

One of the most pleasant times came about when my co-pilot and inseparable friend, Charley Taylor, with my KP help, prepared a meal in the Greenacre's kitchen for the Greenacres. Taylor was a bachelor and quite a good cook. He got Mrs Greenacre's approval to prepare an American southern style meal. The first order of business was to obtain all of the necessary ingredients. Our first stop was the Bedser farmhouse on the air base near our barracks area. We bought two young chickens and prepared them for our purpose. Next stop the flight personnel mess hall and officer's club. Taylor talked the club officer out of potatoes, flour, shortening, salt, pepper and butter. Then on to Halesworth on bicycles. Taylor took "command" and we prepared southern fried chicken, biscuits, milk gravy and mashed potatoes. The milk and a few other ingredients came from Mrs Greenacre's pantry.

When the food was ready to serve, Taylor filled each plate, putting the choicest pieces of chicken on the Greenacre's plates with hot biscuits, mashed potatoes and a generous serving of milk gravy on the biscuits and potatoes. They attempted to cut the meat off the bone with a knife and fork. We stopped them and told them it was an American meal and the chicken should be eaten American style; using fingers instead of a fork. They watched us demonstrate and cautiously took their first bite. From then on it was "gang busters". When the meal was finished there was only a pick of chicken bones and dishes wiped clean with the last of the biscuits.

Mrs Greenacre, in the days following our American style meal, spread the story far and wide in Halesworth. Subsequently we were referred to as "the Yanks who fried chicken". Frying chicken was something the British never did at that time.

Mrs Bedser, from whom we had bought the two chickens for the southern fried feast, often provided us with a farm breakfast of two fresh eggs, buttered toast, jelly and coffee for the price of a half-crown (50 cents). Farmers had advantages in being able to produce foodstuffs which were rationed for the rest of the population, and Mrs Bedser's breakfasts were a welcome change from the food we got on the base. One morning, when we were having breakfast at the farm, Mrs Bedser extended an invitation to us to have lunch with her family on Sunday. We accepted.

Unfortunately, on the Sunday in question we were awakened at 3.00 am to fly a mission. There was no possible way to advise the Bedsers. As soon as the mission was completed and we had been debriefed, Taylor and I went immediately to the Bedser home to apologise. It was about 3.00 pm and we found the whole Bedser family patiently awaiting us. The big surprise was that Mrs Bedser had attempted to prepare a meal of fried chicken, mashed potatoes, biscuits and gravy, all based on Mrs Greenacre's sketchy description. It was all stone cold. Taylor and I forced some of it down, discovering that there was no batter on the chicken and the meal didn't match up to the way a southern dinner should be cooked in several respects. We excused ourselves with a plea of being weary and sleepy after the day's mission. We were somewhat saddened by the disaster as we both were certain that Mrs Bedser had intended to serve us an American chicken dinner and make two American boys feel at home.
Charles Harkins

The English cities weren't that much different from home but out in the real rural areas, oh boy! It was arranged for my friend Elinor and myself to go down to a little village near Salisbury and stay for a short vacation. This was all so strange and quaint to us. I stayed with the local postmaster, whose wife warmed our bed with hot smoothing irons. The place was like an old world picture postcard with a duck pond in the middle and quaint old houses. The local accents were so strong it was like a foreign language to us. We found the village blacksmith. I had always imagined him to be a big man, but this one was a real small guy. When we called in, he took a red hot iron bar from the fire, lit his cigarette and then put the iron back before talking to us. "Oh, you're Americans are you. Do you know my cousin in Chicago?" I think he honestly thought Chicago was a little place like his village.
Helen Maravell

A number of large English country mansions were requisitioned for use as "rest homes: where combat airmen were sent for a week's recuperation. Stanbridge Earls, Romsey, Hampshire was an officers' rest home. While the Americans were in occupation its owner Walter Hutchinson, a publisher, lived in a caravan in the grounds.

There used to be a gnome-like Irishman who came around to the barracks with fresh eggs for sale. One night he appeared with a bottle of Jameson's Irish whiskey, which he sold us for £10. After he had gone we poured ourselves a drink in our mess cups and, to our chagrin, found out it was cold tea. Needless to say we never saw the little Irishman again.
George Collar

Sgt R.E. 'Lefty' Nairn posed by the gate of this old farmhouse at Denham, Suffolk, early in 1945. There was nothing like these old thatched houses in the States. Forty years later, when Lefty returned, Reading Hall had become a smart residence in contrast to the worn look of the war years.   (Lefty Nairn)

We had only been in England a week when the four officers in our crew were given our first pass into Dereham. A taxi was hired and arrangements made with the driver to meet us and get back to Shipdham by midnight; any later and we would be AWOL. Well, the driver never showed up and as it was getting late we went looking for transportation back to camp. There were lots of other Yanks in the same situation trying to find a taxi and we soon found cabs were rare in this small town. Every car that came along was stopped because in the blackout you could not see if it was a cab. The drivers weren't very pleased at being stopped. Some of our fellows were a bit merry and when the driver of one small car cussed us they picked the whole car off the ground then dropped it back. I bet that driver never had a good word for the Yanks after that.

It must have been around 2 am when we finally stopped a car and the driver said it was a cab. Immediately there was a rush to get in and I found myself pushed onto the floor with several other guys on top. The cab driver must have taken fright at the numbers trying to force their way into his cab for he drove off with doors still open to escape the mob. When he got clear and we were able to sort ourselves out I discovered Ira Lee, our navigator, was the only other member of my crew who had been able to get into the overloaded cab. When we got near the base Ira said we better go through the fence as he'd already been caught AWOL earlier in the week and would get into real trouble if caught again. I reminded him we were in a war zone and that the base was patrolled by armed guards who might shoot if they found someone trying to break into the camp during darkness. Ira couldn't be discouraged so we got the cab to stop, paid off the driver and started down the road towards the base, hoping to find a place in the fence where we could squeeze through. Then we heard a vehicle coming up the road from the base gate. 'MPs!' says Ira, 'Better hide.' With that he rushes across the road and vaults over a railing. There is a loud splash and followed by some equally loud cussing. I forgot the MPs and ran to find out what had happened. There was Ira waist deep in a stream trying to catch his hat. I laughed so much we would surely have been caught if it had been an MP's jeep. Instead, when the vehicle passed I saw it was the taxi going back to town after dropping the rest of the men off at the base. We did manage to get into the base and back to our barracks undetected despite the loud squelch from every step my dripping friend made.
Al Jones

Egg hunting. Stopping at any farm you passed and hoping a sympathetic farmer might be persuaded into business. Captain Goldsmith of 3rd Division Hq was unlucky at Babergh Place Farm, Acton in 1944. (Air Force Academy/Mark Brown)

8   MIND THE LANGUAGE

"THEY DON'T speak American round here – and from what I've heard they don't speak English either" was a well-known quip among GIs who found themselves confronted by the obstacles of British accent and vernacular. The United States had its accents but the variations were nowhere near so concentrated as in Britain where it could be notably different in parts of the same county during the early 20th century.

The big troop ships came into the Clyde in Scotland where GIs who had expected no trouble with the language were quickly disillusioned. Arthur Swanson of 357th Fighter Group noted:

> "Most GIs were surprised by the great variation in British accents and the fact that some were so heavy they could not understand what was being said. When we docked at Glasgow we were taken by lighter to a railroad station. While the troops waited for a train a woman came along dispensing tea; she kept calling, 'Gay yer cunten coups oot' and GIs kept asking each other, 'What she say?' Having lived among the Scots community in New York I could translate her request as "Get your canteen cups out."

Fortunately, most of the USAAF were settled in regions of less extreme dialect but there were still difficulties of communication in rural areas. The publican of an inn at Middleton, Suffolk, witnessed an occasion when a friendly GI from the backwoods of Arkansas endeavoured to engage an old farm worker in conversation. It was quickly apparent that both were having difficulty in understanding the other. When the GI had departed the publican enquired of the local what they had discussed and received the disgruntled "buggered if I know. He din't speak our language". The accent expected was that associated with English characters in the movies, the so-called "cultivated" accent. Now the GI was to learn that this was associated with the upper classes, BBC announcers or those who aspired to be "nicely spoken". This dropping of "r" and

use of a broad "a" fascinated some American listeners, particularly if it were drawn out to be really plummy.

Apart from accent there were different pronunciations of certain words. Landgirl Mary Renshaw thought for a moment she was being invited to take part in some act of subversion by a cycling GI who stopped and asked "Can you help me with the rowt?" Her startling introduction to the American pronunciation of route was nothing compared to the shock of a British secretary in an administrative office who was told by a chilled US officer: "Why don't you get your fanny off that chair and shut the darned window." It was some time before she learned that fanny is a perfectly acceptable term for one's rear end in American company.

The different meanings of words in the vernacular of the times was often a source of confusion, embarrassment and amusement. The common British assertion that "I'll knock you up", meaning bang on your door to awaken or alert, was an expression that meant making someone pregnant in common US parlance. GIs were also amused by the expression "keep your pecker up", a request to remain cheerful, but having sexual connotations in their hearing. And surprised looks and sniggers often followed when the British made reference to rubbers. Not a term for erasers in the US.

Misconstrued intentions resulted from some statements. A regular drinker, encountering a GI friend in a pub enquired about the American's usual girlfriend and, on being told "I'm going to have to stand her up", looked about, surprised, and enquired "What, has she had one too many?" Similar ignorance of American expressions resulted in one kind-hearted Hintlesham woman recalling, puzzled, that "Johnny Patton often said he was going to wash up when he'd had a meal with us but he always used to go off to the lavatory and leave us to do it." The significance of "wash up" never did register with this lady.

Slang was another confusing issue in language. The story is told of two airmen having an argument at the bar of the Lavenham *Swan*. The barmaid heard one man say to the other, "You want egg in your beer?" and interjected, "I'm sorry, but I can't do that, eggs are rationed." She was not amused by the mirth engendered until it was explained that "egg in your beer" meant an unreasonable demand. Many were those natives puzzled by such utterances as "Jus bin shooting the breeze", "I'm gonna hit the sack", "How about cuttin' a rug, babe?" Conversely, Americans delighted in mimicking British wartime slang and colloquialisms: "You've had it!" "You can't miss it!" "Good show!"

"Top drawer" "Browned off" "One never knows, does one?", "How's that then!", "I take a dim view", "Actually", "Really?", and "Don't you know there's a war on?" being favourites.

British place names were another problem for the visitor as the phonetical pronunciation was frequently wrong. Railway staff and bus conductors had no difficulty when asked, as they frequently were, for "Nor-which", although sometimes the ticket purchaser would insist it said "Nor-which" on his written orders and not "Norridge". They had more trouble sorting out places such as "Dee-bash" and "Whore-ham" as being "Deb-ige" (Debach) and "Horrum" (Horham).

Speakers' Corner, Hyde Park, London.
Mark Brown/Air Force Academy)

In June 1943, the 389th Bomb Group received orders to proceed to the United Kingdom finally landing at RAF Station Hethel, located immediately adjacent to the village of Wymondham, Norfolk. Upon arrival at the station, the ground crews went to work preparing the aircraft for combat while the aircrews were given a two day stand down to rest after the long flight. Lt H. Ben Walsh, however, had other ideas and hastily made his way to the railway station in the village where he purchased a ticket for London.

After two full days in the big city taking in all the sights, Walsh took the Underground to Liverpool Street station where he joined the normal wartime queue for a return ticket. When his turn finally arrived, Walsh asked for a ticket to "Wy-Mond-Ham". The agent looked perplexed and stated there was no Wy Mond Ham in the British Isles. The young pilot was really taken aback at this statement and had a brief moment of panic. He was certain that his station, Hethel, was located next to the village of Wy Mond Ham. The ticket agent stated he would check with his superiors and determine where the station was really located and left his window. By now Walsh was getting nervous - he was due back on the station for flying the following morning and time was running out. The ticket agent returned shortly and stated Walsh should purchase a ticket for "Windem" which was near "Norich". By now this poor Yank was ready to accept any answer and if this would get him to his station, so be it. Needless to say he arrived at the proper destination but the incident convinced Walsh that the British had their own King's English and it did not necessarily follow the American pronunciation.
H. Ben Walsh

As a gesture towards promoting Anglo-American goodwill the Mayor of Peterborough arranged for me to spend a weekend at the Marlborough Head Inn at a picturesque place called Dedham near Colchester. While there I met Edgar Cooper and his wife, farmers from a nearby village, with whom I became lifelong friends. I subsequently made other visits to Dedham when I had leave and the Coopers introduced me to many of their friends. One evening a couple, relatives of the Coopers, were present. I enjoyed their company and hoped to expand on the friendship at a later date. With this in mind, when the couple came to leave, instead of wishing them good night I tossed an American flip: "I'll see you later." Unfortunately they took this to mean that I was going to visit them later that night in their home. After sitting around until 3.00am they went to bed, probably with some pretty hard thoughts about Americans who said they would visit but didn't show up. When I heard about this I bought an American to English and English to American dictionary, but I was a long time getting their friendship back!
Nelson Matthews

Captain Nelson Matthews, a lead bombardier (right) with friend Captain Smith from the 351st Bomb Group and Edgar Cooper at the latter's Little Bromley, Essex farm.

One time, in London by myself looking for a good place to eat, I went into one of the major hotels. As I went by the doors there were a couple of our MPs walking up and down the street. I sat down and was about to order when a waiter comes over and says, "There's an MP who would like you to join him." Well the first thing I thought of was the two MPs I'd seen out there, so I said I don't want anything to do with MPs and if they want they can come and talk to me. The waiter went away and didn't approach me again. I had my meal and left. I got to wondering why an MP should want me. It was only later that someone suggested that the MP was a British Member of Parliament. I've often wondered what I missed and that I might have left a bad impression of GIs' courtesy if it was a British politician.
Wilbur Richardson

SINCE the Second World War a somewhat prejudiced and exaggerated picture of the relationship between white and coloured US troops in Britain has been created by investigative journalists looking for racial injustices. Overall, the relationships between black and white were reasonably harmonious. Frictions and disturbances between the races were no more marked than those between caucasian GIs themselves, or those involving British and other Allied personnel. Soon after arriving in the UK as European Theater of Operations Commander, General Eisenhower declared that he would not tolerate discrimination towards black soldiers, a policy actively pursued by the USAAF commanders, Generals Spaatz and Eaker. However, at lower levels in the chain of command some officers did not give the matter the attention it deserved and problems did arise. The deep-seated feelings held by men from the southern states in the aftermath of the American civil war were still prevalent in many of the generation that served in the military 80 years later. Of particular abhorrence to them was the sight of white girls associating with negroes, something not seen in the South back home. Many of the incidents that occurred could be traced to this aversion.

The ethnic minorities in the UK prior to 1945 amounted to a very small proportion of the population and coloured people were rarely seen except in very localised areas. In consequence the British were devoid of pronounced racial consciousness; coloured people were not a threat to their accepted society. There was a genial attitude towards black servicemen, who were generally considered well-behaved, polite and dignified. Many English girls enjoyed the company of these coloured GIs, particularly at dances. It was competition for local girls during a dance at Thurston in December 1942 that sparked a confrontation between white GIs from a nearby airfield and men from the negro truck company based at Troston Park,

Private Elco Bolton from Florida seeks directions from a Bobby. 30 June 1942. (Imperial War Museum)

Suffolk. As a result of intimidation, a negro lieutenant was sufficiently alarmed to arm his men. Calm was eventually restored without violence.

Six months later an uglier incident occurred at the Quartermaster Truck depot at Bamber Bridge, Lancashire, while in Ipswich military police arrested two GIs who were openly threatening to arrange to beat up all coloured soldiers seen with white women. Negro GIs were probably unduly sensitive to the question of racial discrimination and over-reacted in some of these incidents. General Ira Eaker, commander of the 8th Air Force, considered that 90 per cent of the trouble was the fault of whites. Thereafter a more strenuous effort was made to avoid further incidents of this kind. A degree of segregation was introduced for leisure activities at the discretion of local commanders, who appointed some "on pass" towns for whites and others for blacks. Similarly, in other towns certain places of entertainment, particularly public houses, were out of bounds to whites on some nights and to blacks on others. This proved reasonably successful and only the isolated minor incident occurred during the remainder of the war, although some Southerners never did come to terms with black personnel walking out with English girls.

The first black units for the USAAF arriving in June 1942 were members of engineer companies. These and following arrivees were quickly engaged in the airfield building programme in Suffolk and Essex. One oft told anecdote of the time is said to have originated at *The Dog Inn*, Grundisburgh, near the site where Debach

airfield was being constructed. When a visiting journalist asked an aged yokel what he thought of the Americans in the area, the old boy put down the pint he was quaffing, thought a minute and replied: "Reckon they're all right; but I don't think much of these white fellers they brought with 'em." Most USAAF negro units were Quartermaster Truck and Ordnance Ammunition Companies engaged in hauling supplies, bombs and ammunition from depots to combat bases and other non-combat duties. The total number of black GIs in the UK did not reach 10,000 until 1944, with a peak of 12,000 the following year.

Coloured soldiers served in most of the supply depots dotted around England. At this "thank you" get-together with British ladies from voluntary organisations, a form of segregation is noticeable in that black GIs are not seated at the same tables as white GIs. (via Vic Lewis)

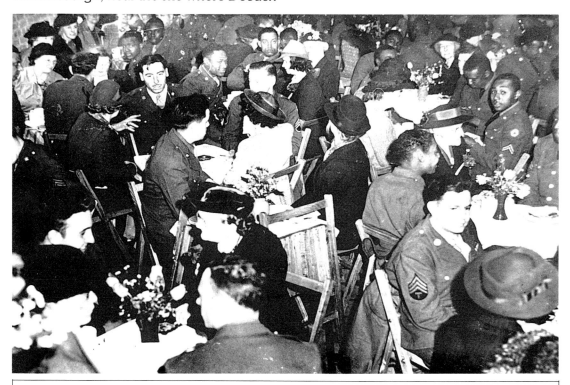

Amiable relations with the British, servicemen and civilians, were a high priority factor for 8th Air Force Staffs and of primary concern to the Public Relations Officers (PROs). After all, we Yanks were foreigners on their island. Generally these relations were quite friendly with a good deal of give and take on both sides. Some conflicts were unavoidable but there probably were almost as many incidents between Yanks as between Yanks and British. Anticipation and prevention of untoward happenings were paramount.

In this vein, our PRO Bill Laidlaw was becoming increasingly concerned with a potential racial problem. The 97th Bomb Group occupied Polebrook, just a few miles from the small town of Oundle. By early August 1942 the ground crews and, as the B-17s arrived, the air crews "took over"' the town. The pubs and other public facilities became their hang-outs and a warm welcome was afforded the lasses of the town. All was serene until in mid-September a Quartermaster truck unit occupied a facility near Northampton, some 18 miles distant. The unit was manned largely by coloured (negro) drivers while a majority of the 97th Group personnel came from our southern states. As could be expected, it wasn't too long after liberty was granted that the truckers started to infiltrate the facilities of Oundle, much to the resentment of 97th Group members. A few fights and minor disturbances took place.

PRO Bill was following these events closely and, after discussions with Wing and Group staffs, scheduled a mid October meeting between the Group Executive officer, several unit commanders and executives and the Mayor and officials of Oundle. The one o'clock lunch, hosted by the Mayor, consisted of starch weighted, wartime food with a treacle pudding dessert. At around 2.30 the meeting convened in the City chambers. The day was quite warm for October, windows were open, not a breath of air was stirring and a few flies were buzzing.

Bill led off the affair. In concise and succinct terms he reviewed the historical and developmental background of Southern attitudes, touched upon the current happenings and possible results in Oundle, and inquired of the Mayor and Council their views. There was some discussion and comment but nothing cogent or constructive was offered.

Bill then increased emphasis, reviewing some of the US racial events, summarized again the current situation, and again appealed to the Mayor and Council. Viewing the audience he noted the Mayor and several of the Council seemed to be nodding and some of the Yanks did not seem to be too alert. He then decided to "Pour it on". With rising voice he appealed to his audience:

"Your Honor, Mr Mayor, Council Members and fellow officers, what I am trying to present is this: With your over 1000 year old town, your 11th Century church, the 12th Century Boys School, your tradition, your culture, your centuries old public and private buildings, your provincial heritage and small town environment; Mr Mayor and Council, what I am trying my best to bring home to you is -- What will be the impact on your town, with its long traditions, when the first BLACK baby is born here???"

For a brief interval, silence prevailed whereon the Mayor straightened his shoulders and stated, "Why Captain, I think it would be the Pet of the Town!!"

Though little substantive was resolved at this meeting, certain agreements, mostly between the US units, were formulated and few other untoward incidents occurred. This at least partly resulted from the 97th Group departure in November for the North African Campaign.

As a footnote to the above, about one year later, a 'Black Baby' was born in Northampton, its mother paraded it via pram in the public areas *and it was the pet of the town*.

Tom Morrow

When the 1514th Quartermaster Company of coloured GIs arrived at Broughton, Northamptonshire, their parade through Kettering was filmed by British Pathe News. They are seen here marching down Gold Street with one of their white officers. (Quenton Bland)

10   OVERPAID?

THE CRUELLEST, yet most enduring comment on the American invasion of 1942-45 was the quip, "The trouble with the Yanks is they're overpaid, oversexed and over here." Sometimes expanded with the addition of "overfed" or "overbearing", its origin was supposedly the repartee of a comedian at a munitions factory workers' show. The saying has been quoted so frequently that - apart from being hackneyed – it has come to represent the general view of the British about their ally during those war years which, in truth, was certainly not the case.

The GI was not overpaid; his British counterpart was underpaid, particularly the lower ranks. In 1944 the basic rate for the lowest grade of US private in the UK was £3 15s ($15) a week, whereas the ordinary RAF airman received £17s 6d ($3.50); the American having more than four times as much in his pocket. There were various allowances and deductions, notably a 50% increase for men on flying duty. Thus a Staff Sergeant air gunner on a B-17 or B-24 bomber would receive £10 15s ($43) a week, which was still about four times the pay an RAF sergeant with equivalent duties would receive. The pay differences were not so marked among officers, with, for example, a US Captain on flying duties receiving about twice that of RAF Flight Lieutenant. Although all US Army rank payments were higher than British, the difference narrowed the higher the rank.

The situation was bound to cause resentment among British servicemen, being placed in an inferior position in their own homeland. The GI could spend lavishly, affording things such as taxi journeys which were out of reach of British lower ranks. Above all, his deeper pocket gave the GI an advantage with the womenfolk. The resentment that arose was further fuelled by the GI's access to goods scarce or unobtainable in Britain through the PX stores. The US airman was also better clad than his British counterpart, having a much superior cloth to that used in Battle Dress. British Army "other ranks" did not even have a tie for walking out in uniform until late in the war. Officer issue was more equal and where the British could afford the services of a civilian tailor their officers were often better turned out.

A good amount of envy and jealousy existed where US servicemen were concerned for the foregoing reasons, to which could be added a tinge of resentment that Uncle Sam appeared to be taking over the direction of the war effort. Some British servicemen never ceased to nurse a grudge against the "bloody Yanks", the United States and Americans being a convenient scapegoat for disillusion and troubles. Conversely, some US servicemen did not hide personal considerations of their ally as an inferior being. Hostility did show itself in pub brawls and hard words. Such incidents were the exception, for overall the relationship between the armed forces of the two nations was good and a great many lasting friendships were made. Contact between individuals usually melted prejudice and prompted understanding, and as the fighting capability of the US forces became evident this brought a new respect. The high commands, sensitive to the American serviceman's advantages, took various steps to promote harmony. British goodwill was at its best with the RAF who were facing the same perils. The bond that arose between the combat airmen of the RAF and USAAF was evident by the treatment accorded those flyers of one force who arrived on one of the other's airfields, as Technical Sergeant Leon Senk's experience shows.

"We had to crash-land at an RAF fighter base in southern England coming back from Chemnitz in March 1945. The people on the field really went out of their way for us. We were provided with shaving gear and towels for us to clean up. The mess hall was closed but they opened it up for us. The cooks asked what we'd like to eat: I said, I'm dying for liver and onions and that's what I got. We ate real good. When we'd finished we each pitched in a pound note for the cook ... gladly."

As the cook's tip amounted to a month's wages, such generosity can only have left a favourable impression. This was probably another example of confusion over money values. However, many Americans, sensitive to the fact that they were paid considerably more than their British buddies, were deliberately benevolent. An RAF officer, serving in a liaison capacity at one USAAF installation, found the generosity sincere, if embarrassing, as he could not respond in kind. He eventually came to terms with the situation, appreciating that his American friends truly did not expect reciprocal favours.

The possibility of friction between the servicemen of Britain and the United States was quickly seized upon by the Nazi propaganda machine which used leaflets and radio broadcasts in attempts to promote dissension. The main thrust of this propaganda was to provoke concern amongst British forces overseas by presenting a picture of wives and sweethearts falling prey to amorous and free-spending Yanks. Propaganda aimed at GIs in Britain centred on exploitation by those around them and the implication that every military move was betrayed by Britons sympathetic to the German cause. Like UK residents, Americans tuned their radios to Lord Haw-Haw, the German-English broadcast, for amusement. Strangely, a persistent rumour among USAAF personnel was that the arrival and fortunes of individual units frequently featured in these transmissions, but there is no recorded evidence to substantiate even one of these supposed statements.

The more relaxed situation between officers and men in the US forces was seen as a lack of discipline by British officers, and there is no denying that the conduct of many GIs appeared casual compared to the regimented ranks of the British Army. The division between US officers and men was certainly not so marked. An amusing illustration of the British view comes from an attempt by the local Home Guard at Boxted, Essex to establish good relations with the USAAF 354th Fighter Group that had recently moved into the nearby airfield. The group commander and his staff were invited to a dinner, together with British Army officers from Colchester garrison. A retired General of First World War distinction and Empire service accepted a request to address the gathering. All went

well until the old General rose, when much to the embarrassment of the hosts and guests he launched into criticism of US troops he had seen. Any soldiers in his command who slouched, hands in pockets, with tunic buttons undone and improperly dressed would have been quickly put on a charge, he asserted in his tirade. Then he stopped; a broad grin spreading across his face, and continued, "But you can't help liking the buggers, can you?!"

Sgt Earl Robinson and a British soldier, exchanged headgear as a gesture of goodwill when a friend wanted to take a snap.
(Earl Robinson)

In 1938 I began to write to a pen-friend, Miss Joan Green, in Leeds, Yorkshire. After a year or two we lost contact. However, Joan's address stayed somewhere in the back of my mind and after I arrived in the UK and became settled in at Debach in September 1944, I wrote Joan, knowing she probably wondered what had become of me as the war unfolded. She and her mother both wrote back urging me to come to Leeds at the first opportunity. There was much hesitation because I knew about rationing in England, besides which the rail connections were very vague. There were no regular advertised schedules, probably for security reasons. I finally decided to give it a try and, after the first time, made the trip frequently, but I never got to Leeds by the same route twice! When I boarded the train at Ipswich it was with the understanding that the conductor would tell me where to get off to make the first connection. Then in the next station I'd ask someone which train to get on and the next conductor would tell me where to get off again, and so on to Leeds.

On one occasion in the bitter cold winter of 1944-45 I had an interesting encounter. It was so cold that at each stop I would buy a cup of tea and two or three of those hard little cookies or crackers. The tea wasn't just to drink, by holding the cup between my hands I could warm them as there was no heating in the carriages. On one leg of the journey I found myself in a compartment with a young RAF sergeant. His insignia indicated he was an aircrew member and I immediately felt that I had a friend. However, I tried without success to strike up conversation. He would only answer my questions with a very curt, "Yes" or "No". At the next station we both changed trains and I heard him mention that he was going to the Bradford area. I knew Bradford was near Leeds so I stuck to the young sergeant like wallpaper – you better believe I was having a hard time with the English accents trying to understand directions.

When we set off again there was an older man sitting opposite us in the compartment who noticed my attempts to engage the RAF sergeant in conversation. He explained that British enlisted personnel do not converse with officers except to answer questions and then as briefly as possible. This older man then pointed out to the young sergeant that the Yank was trying to be friendly and that he, the sergeant, was not being properly polite. The RAF man relaxed after that and was soon all smiles. He proved to be as curious about the 8th Air Force as I was about RAF Bomber Command. He was a Lancaster gunner and had completed a tour of duty but was hoping that his pilot could pull a few strings so that he could remain on operations. He felt that if he was grounded he might end up in "the pits" – the coal mines, which I assume was his peacetime job. He was fascinated by our going to targets in broad daylight while I couldn't imagine milling around in darkness in the midst of other aircraft. We talked about how interesting it would be to trade places for one mission.

As the journey wore on it became apparent that at the rate of progress we were making I was not going to arrive in Leeds until two or three o'clock in the morning. I asked if anyone in the compartment might recommend a hotel close to the rail station. Immediately a woman said that there should be no need to find a hotel as she was sure that any householder to whom I explained my predicament would be happy to find me a bed for the night, further suggesting that when I got to Leeds I should "knock someone up". I was momentarily taken aback by this statement as in American slang it means making someone pregnant. This was the first time I had heard this expression from a Britisher but quickly realised that the woman was telling me to go bang on a door. At the same time my new-found RAF friend invited me to go home with him if I didn't mind getting off at Bradford, taking a bus with him to a smaller place and a mile walk. He pressed me but I had to decline. I knew how few rations these people got. For example, my friends the Greens had nine people in their home and could only buy two eggs a week. I was also aware that the sergeant's family was not aware he was coming on leave and I could picture the scene when he arrived, unexpectedly in the wee hours with a Yank in tow. His offer was appreciated more than he probably realised but I begged off on the grounds that my leave time was too short, which was true. That night was spent at the Queens Hotel, an act for which Mrs Green scolded me soundly when I arrived next day. Felt badly about the RAF man's offer as I probably hurt his feelings in declining. Wish I had gotten his name and address and I often wonder if he survived the air war.

John Ramsey

Below left: Joan Green and Lt John Ramsey outside 42 Alexandra Road, Leeds; December 1944.

Below right: Civilians are few and far between in this view down Shaftesbury Avenue towards Piccadilly Circus in 1945. Allied servicemen abound and the majority are American. (via Bruce Robertson)

11 OVERSEXED?

Typical of the unofficial artwork on USAAF aircraft is *Double Trouble*, a Liberator that flew from Rackheath, Norfolk.

AN ASPECT of the Second World War American servicemen in the UK that became legend was his amorous nature. In fact, he was no more "oversexed" than any other young man removed from home influences and serving in the military. The legend is undoubtedly due to the GI's forthright and open attitude towards sexual matters, together with their overt preoccupation with girls. Indeed, it was the GI who introduced the now major connotation of the word sex, which at the time simply meant gender to British people. Yet another facet of the scene was the extraordinary contrast between the well advertised puritan morality of the United States that to the British reflected a nature far more strait-laced than their own, and the open activities of the young men in their midst.

The prudish censorship applied to motion pictures, the press and elsewhere in the United States was an Establishment stance by religious influence. In reality, a much more liberal attitude to sexual matters prevailed in ordinary society than in Britain, where the subject was "not very nice", and, generally, something one did not speak about. The UK's wartime armed forces were well divorced from this with their "barrack room" language based on sexual profanity. The US military were similarly vocal in promoting sexual acts, which had the effect of conditioning men to "have a good time". Background, of course, still had the major influence on conduct and most men were not hell-bent on seeking sexual experience. Nevertheless, in any large unit there were uninhibited individuals who saw nothing shameful in associating with prostitutes, whereas this would have been an extremely rare admission from a British man of similar inclination.

Prostitution in the UK certainly flourished with the presence of the GI. The oldest profession was not illegal, although soliciting for custom was. In "red light" areas of big cities the police, having more pressing business, were inclined to turn a blind eye to discreet soliciting. However, Piccadilly Commandos were famous for their brazen approaches. With knowledge of the US serviceman's pay, doorway tariff rose from 5/- to 10/- or more if there was no inclination for the customer to barter, while "£5 and breakfast" was usual for an overnight stay in an apartment. While London's West End harboured the greatest concentrations of prostitutes, they were to be found in most provincial towns near US military bases. USAAF records mention a blonde (supposedly serving in the WAAF) who resided near Bury St Edmunds airfield and charged £2 for each favour to airmen of the base. At Colchester, one enterprising girl regularly hired a taxi to take her services to local airfields, having discovered that it was possible to enter isolated parts of the camps by crossing a few fields. Her income must have been considerable as the taxi always waited to convey her back to town. Prostitutes and the helplessly promiscuous were drawn to parties on US bases and though the authorities made some effort to ban these undesirables it was difficult. There are several recorded cases of girls being ejected from barracks where they had been sheltered for several days following station parties. One veteran recalls a girl hidden in his Nissen hut for two weeks and then only discovered by the military police after most of its occupants had failed to return from a disastrous bomber mission.

It is understandable that young men who knew that the odds against surviving a combat tour were slim might wish to "have a good time" but the majority of promiscuous adventurerers were ground men if venereal disease statistics are an indicator. VD infections rose dramatically, doubling in many units after a few months in Britain. The worst incidence in the 8th Air Force for several months in 1944 was the bomb group based at Kimbolton which also had the best operational record of all similar organisations in the Command. The high incidence is surprising in view of the well advertised availability of prophylactic kits for soldiers "going on pass".

The availability of contraceptives and the knowledge that the PX sold such items as nylon stockings, cosmetics and scented soaps led to a suspicion among the British that the US authorities were blatantly encouraging their men to seduce UK womanhood. Rumour being what it is, airmen in training in the USA gained the impression from returned veterans that European girls were "easier" than those at home and could be wooed with scented soaps and other feminine delights unavailable over there. However, would-be seducers found that the scene was not what they had been led to believe; chastity before marriage was as important to girls in Britain as in the United States. Most sexual adventurers were soon made aware of this; but a girl had to watch her step and not invite trouble as Rose Searah, who lived at Chatham, Kent describes:

> "I think the officers were the worst; they expected payment if they gave you a good time. When you met them at dances they'd often ask you if you would like a day out in London when they next went there on pass. If you accepted they would wine and dine you like you'd never known before and then they would somehow miss the last train home. Next thing they'd be offering to get a room for the night in a hotel. The girl had either to accept or stick it out on a cold station till the morning. It depended on the girl; some gave in to temptation. My mother always cautioned me not to accept gifts from Americans because eventually I'd be presented with the bill."

The Second World War had a profound effect on a large proportion of young British women who volunteered for the services and essential war work, or were conscripted. It gave them a new-found freedom and liberation from parental influence and the usual pattern of female conformity. The uncertainty of life in the war years added to this release. The coming of the GI added yet another dimension; these young men's brashness made them exciting, part of the Hollywood image come true. This could later have led to disillusion but the girls found that once one got to know these young men, most were kind, courteous and fun. Additionally, by most accounts, they were more romantically inclined than British boys; sentimental charmers. They certainly had something special, for an estimated 60,000 British women married American servicemen.

As traditionally it is the man who proposes, what attracted the American male? Perhaps the reasons postulated by a

Right: Elizabeth Shapley, a pretty Bedford 17 year-old, who was voted the "Squadron Sweetheart" by the 423rd Bomb Squadron at Thurleigh in January 1945, had a Fortress named *Elizabeth's Own* in her honour. Colonel James Sutton, the station commander, was on hand at the christening ceremony. (The bottle of champagne was heavily diluted!) Elizabeth later married a US officer from another station.

Far right: Lt Colonel Immanuel Klette, who flew 91 combat missions with the 8th Air Force, more than any other bomber pilot, met his bride while in hospital recovering from severe wounds sustained in a crash. Lt Margaret "Peg" Kerns was one of "Manny's" nurses.

Fighter pilot, Captain Earl Abbot married Florence DeLuce, a Red Cross nurse at Bodney. The CO, Colonel Joe Mason, and his friend, Lady Joan Huntingfeld (left), posed with the newlyweds in the grounds of Clermont Hall.

thrice-married former officer who did not include a British bride in that experience is enlightening: "You saw more good looking, shapely girls in England than you did in the States or other European countries where I was stationed. They had by far the best legs and complexions. We had already spoilt our women; set them up too high. The English girls, by contrast, were far more feminine with softer personalities and more sympathetic towards a man."

One suspects that attraction was enhanced on both sides by the excitement of being involved with a person of another nationality, an added piquancy to exploration of the unknown. One thing is sure, the majority of the 60,000 young men did not set out to acquire a British wife on arrival; the dream was still the girl back home. Initially all that was sought was female company, to get to know what British girls were like and with no firm sexual objective either. Just to have fun.

The first step was to make contact and the average GI was not bashful when it came to introductions. Sometimes the objectives were not very co-operative, as co-pilot Bud Chamberlain discovered.

"On a bright July afternoon another pilot and I set out from Halesworth on our bicycles to visit friends at Bungay. When we got on to the long straight road that runs between the two little towns we saw two girls on bikes ahead of us. Now there was an opportunity to get us a little female company on our trip so we set off to

overtake them. We pedalled as hard as we could but those girls stayed way ahead of us for miles. In the end we had to admit defeat and that English girls were too fast for us Yanks!"

No doubt the young ladies concerned were apprehensive of Yanks, about whom dire warnings circulated among the indigenous population of the land. Tales of rapes and other horrors, mostly false and exaggerated with each re-telling, made some girls nervous of any contact with GIs. There were also reports of minor indignities, generally the result of harmless fooling, such as the prank played by Warren Hill and his buddies at Bassingbourn:

"Our hardstand was right beside the Royston-Cambridge highway. Most mornings girls would cycle past on their way to work. Often we'd be pre-flighting our B-17 *Vertigo* for a mission. When we saw the girls coming we'd have the engines idling. As soon as they reached directly behind the aircraft we'd crack up the power and try to blow up their skirts. Nearly blew two right off their cycles one morning."

Direct approaches in the street were quite common and while the GI saw nothing untoward in this, it was not the way a nice British girl would expect an introduction to be made and would have immediately been put on her guard. The "Hi Babe! Hows about you and me getting together?" approach usually earned the

Where there were Yanks there were girls. These officers from Shipdham enjoy a day at the seaside, 1943. (William Cameron)

cold shoulder. Some persevered as Iris Falcone relates:

"My first experience of Americans was that they were extremely cheeky, very forward, not at all like British boys; but they were extremely friendly. The way I met my husband was in a Peterborough restaurant. My friend and I had gone in for afternoon tea before work. At the next table were three American servicemen and they started to eye us. We thought they were trying to pick us up so, being well brought up English girls, we would have nothing whatever to do with them. About a month later, when we were back at the same restaurant for tea, one of the American boys who had sat next to us on the previous occasion came in. He marched right over to our table and before we could say yes, no or maybe, he sat down and introduced himself. We were quite taken aback, a British boy would never have pushed in like that. His name was Joseph and my friend thought he was smashing, while I thought he was extremely rude. I didn't encourage him but he found out from my friend that we both worked at the Embassy Theatre. From then on he haunted the Embassy until I finally gave in and dated him. I don't think my mother thought it would turn into anything serious, in fact she said on several occasions why not bring these American boys home to tea, they are away from their homes and families and must get quite lonely. So we had Joseph and some of his friends on numerous occasions and mother really took to him; thought him the best of the lot. I didn't think that way but eventually his courting won out and I married him."

The obvious place to make contact with girls was dance halls and the GIs found plenty in the UK. Apart from the regular every night dance halls in big towns and cities, dances were a regular feature of smaller public halls – and many village halls had one every Saturday night. In all the GIs soon began to influence behaviour. Foxtrot and waltzes were reduced to a close in shuffle with one's partner which ballroom dancing enthusiasts criticised as being an excuse for a mobile embrace. Quicksteps brought the jitterbugging exponents onto the floor and many a girl discovered that "let's cut a rug Honey" was not an invitation to get to work on a carpet with a pair of scissors. There were some aspects of the British dance hall scene that were strange to GIs, as Al Zimmerman of 493rd Bomb Group found:

"The place to go in London to dance was

The prominence of "pin-ups" in USAAF barracks and the girly paintings on aircraft all helped to enhance the Americans' supposed preoccupation with young women. Pages from magazines and calendars adorn the wall behind Major James Goodson's bed in his Debden quarters. This very distinguished fighter ace lost his heart to an English girl and would choose to live in the UK in later years.

the converted opera house near Covent Garden. It was here that I first took the floor with a British gal. All was going fine until another girl tried to cut in, grabbed me by the arm and tried to pull me away. I'd been told the English girls were shy and reserved and here's one trying to pull me away from another! Embarrassed, I just held on to the girl I had, said 'How do you do' and kept dancing. My partner's immediate reaction was offence; what was I doing not taking the other girl? I was bewildered until it was explained that this was a ladies' 'Excuse Me' dance. When a girl tapped your shoulder you changed partners."

While the majority of dance attendees were just young men who wanted to meet girls and have fun, there is no doubt that the halls attracted those with sexual motives. Nancy Ruska's experience was not uncommon, although to be fair, while American soldiers tended to be the main servicemen "tarred with this brush" they were not the only amorous predators at such functions:

"Dances were the big events in our lives in Hethersett as it must have been for most village girls. There were lots of American servicemen at these dances and it was noticeable that they paid a lot of attention to particular girls. I was very young and innocent and, as a dare with some other girls, I got one of the Americans to dance with me whom I knew was going with one popular girl. That was nearly my downfall; he must have thought I was leading him on. He asked if he could take me home. It was a bit early and I didn't want to go yet but, for some silly reason, I agreed. We didn't get too far down the road before he wanted to take me into a place we called Kissing Alley. There I almost got more than kissing. He got hold of my wrists and held them so tight I couldn't move. I was frightened and told him that if he didn't let go I'd scream. He didn't, so I screamed, and then he let go. The incident really scared me and I was a lot more careful after that."

Dances were the frequent starting point for relationships but perhaps as many that resulted in permanence came about in a variety of other ways, so often characterised by the young man's persistence after a first sighting, a normal entry into courtship the world over. Jordan Utal, an officer with 2nd Air Division Headquarters, describes his persistence:

"Riding my Raleigh bike on the way to lunch at the Horsham St Faith mess, I saw a very attractive blonde girl in civilian clothes

Womens' Land Army girls from the Culford hostel in Suffolk enjoy an evening's dancing with GIs. The girls' uniforms did nothing for a feminine appearance but a sizeable number of Land Girls married US servicemen. (Imperial War Museum)

come out of the Red Cross office. Having taken note, when I got to the mess I found one of the American Red Cross girls to ask who this attractive blonde I had seen might be. When told she was Joyce, an English girl working for the Field Director, I said that I'm in love already. She asked what I meant and I told her that I came from New York and when young, as my family didn't own a car, I only dated girls who lived no more than ten blocks away from my home. But for this one I'd make an exception. She laughed and said she didn't know if she could get me a date but would try. So she told Joyce about this love-smitten fellow, who laughed and said that she couldn't be bothered. Cupid's lot is not easily cast off so I suggested to the Red Cross girl, Jean Marshall, that if she brought a date I could invite Joyce to make up a foursome for dinner. She agreed and I phoned Joyce at her office and she accepted my invitation. Jean Marshall's date happened to be a young Captain who within a year became one of the top fighter aces in England. Joyce and I dated regularly after that and

The Lecture Hall at Sawston. The 66th Fighter Wing's own quartet, the Bobcats, played at the dances. (via B. Robertson)

Passion Waggons was the popular name for the US trucks that brought girls from surrounding towns and villages to Saturday night dances at the local bases. These vehicles are parked near Thetford rail station boarding girls for Knettishall and East Wretham airfields.

married 17 months later. I'm glad I made an exception to the ten block rule; the smartest move I made in my whole life."

This resulted in a marriage that "could not have been happier", sentiments echoed by Bill Barnett of 384th Bomb Group who sees coincidence as an important factor that brought him and his wife together:

"Not many people can bless the day they broke a foot, but I can. Some horseplay during cadet pilot training resulted in this injury, putting me two months behind the rest of my class. Most went to Italy but I eventually ended up at Grafton Underwood, England. Shortly after my arrival I attended a dance and noticed a pretty girl on her own who appeared to be somewhat uncomfortable. After asking her to dance and getting acquainted, it turned out she had been stood up by another Grafton airman. I then started bicycle missions to Kettering nearly every evening. Couple of weeks later she found out that the man who dated her for the dance hadn't shown up because he broke his foot that afternoon and was in the base hospital. So one broken foot sent me to Grafton Underwood and another broken foot started a partnership that resulted in four children, seven grandchildren, and on."

Approval for an Anglo-American marriage was by no means easy, particularly in the girl's case. Most parents were not eager to

see a daughter entwined with a man from a faraway land, of whose background they knew little and when what they had been told could rarely be confirmed. This protectiveness was strong enough in some cases to prevent the union and in others it took time before parents came to terms with the prospect. Cecilia Trip, the English half of a happy marriage, had her father making the initial move:

"Daddy met him somewhere and invited him to call, but failed to advise Mummy of the fact. One evening this Yank comes knocking on our front door wanting to know if Mr Smith was home. No, but we expected Daddy shortly if he would care to come in and wait. He did, and showed up the eight following evenings. It was quickly obvious that Daddy wasn't the attraction. The relationship developed steadily but when we decided to marry Daddy wasn't very happy. I was the only child and he didn't like the thought of me going to America which seemed so remote from England in those days of long sea journeys. But Daddy had no one to blame but himself; he was the one who had invited the Yank home!"

No doubt many American mothers were apprehensive on hearing their sons had taken a British bride but the principal caution, which almost amounted to opposition in the early days, was expressed by the US authorities. This manifested itself at unit level with the prospective bridegroom being interviewed by the CO or his delegate and the base chaplain of the man's denomination. The pitfalls of such a proposed alliance were pointed out and the soldier asked to think again. The girl also had to have an interview with the base chaplain and, if she were of another religious denomination to her intended husband, this could be particularly hard. When the trickle of marriages became a flood these interviews mellowed considerably. Robert Cayer was faced with the official attitude that existed in 1942:

> "I was one of the first men at Bassingbourn to have an English bride. I didn't drink and was having tea and sandwiches at some function in a church hall and got talking to a girl in British Army uniform, the ATS. When I asked for a date she backed off and said that I better write her a letter to ask! Never met such a shy girl. Well, eventually she accepted my proposal of marriage but the chaplain was told to try and talk me out of it. Don't think the US Army was too keen on its men marrying foreign girls at that time. To complicate matters I was Catholic and my future wife Protestant. In the end the chaplain was convinced I knew what I was doing and said go ahead. The chaplain on my wife's ATS base also had a long talk with her."

GIs who married usually only had contact with wives when on leave. Those members of ground personnel on "permanent" stations were more fortunate and when not on duty were permitted to live off base. Marion Smith of the 4th Strategic Air Depot was one:

> "Got married in October 1944 and we had a room in my wife's sister's house in Sproughton Road, Ipswich. Providing I was in by 7 o'clock in the morning I was allowed the spend the night off base. It was about 10 miles from the Hitcham depot to where my wife lived and for the rest of my time in England I cycled there after coming off duty and back each morning. The trip took about an hour and in the cold and the blackout it wasn't easy."

Wives of air crew were less fortunate, apart from the concern for the loved one's safety – and several girls became widows – the tours of duty were often short, with the airmen having to return to the USA long before the end of hostilities, leaving wives behind. One can only speculate on the number of amorous friendships that did not end in marriage; probably many

thousands. Apart from the obvious, differing degrees of mutual affection, a not uncommon obstacle was religious backgrounds. Stanley Sajdak relates:

> "For a time I went with an English girl called Doris and she took me to her home. Her parents had me to meals and I could see this was putting a strain on their rations. Her father cut the roast in slices that were not much thicker than paper. So I used to try and take something from the base every time I visited. I'd smuggle out gallon cans of pineapple or spam in my knapsack. As you can guess, this made me popular. After a few weeks, when we were alone, Doris's father asked me what my intentions were towards his daughter. 'Honorable', I told him, but how could I tell him that you don't take a non-Catholic English bride home to a Polish mother."

Unusual is the situation to which Roy Winn became sensitive:

> "I started dating a girl who lived around 20 miles south-west from our base at Deenethorpe, a good distance when the transportation available was a bike. As Group Bombardier and a Captain I was able to pull a little rank and get pilots on local flights to land at Harrington, a base near her home. I'd jump out with my overnight bag and Jean would meet me outside the airfield with two bicycles. I discovered that her father was a local squire, a gentleman farmer who owned land in the area. The family had five satellite farms and Jean and I would ride out on horses with bread and newspapers in our saddlebags for these places. She was a great girl but I came to realize that she and her family were my intellectual and social superiors. Although they always made me welcome and treated me fine I was conscious of my background, lack of education and different lifestyle. I was a first generation American, my folk having come from north-east England where my relations still worked as miners and on other manual jobs. This wouldn't worry most Americans but I guess I was too close to my roots not to be class conscious. Jean and her people didn't worry about my background; it was just me. I planned to go to college after the war and come back to England. But with separation we both went different ways and married other people. Even so, we have always kept in touch and remain the very best of friends."

Although North American womanhood reached the UK, romances with GIs did not blossom on anything like the scale of those with the indigenous female popu-

Fighter pilot Walker
Mahurin checks out the
latest pin-ups in 56th
Fighter Group
Operations.

lation. Approximately 10,000 US women passed through or were stationed in the UK, the total comprising some 4,500 WACs, a similar number of Army nurses and around 1,000 Red Cross employees. The first WAC battalion, 700 strong, arrived in July 1943 and its personnel were assigned to a wide variety of duties at Command Headquarters level. Internal resistance to women in the US armed services had led to an overly cautious attitude to their enrolment. At some levels

in Washington the idea prevailed that the undesirable elements of female society would be drawn to the WAC. In reality the reverse was the case; the average WAC was a capable individual and from a good home. Helen Maravell who served at Bushey Hall, Watford comments:

"We were the first WAC battalion sent overseas and had very thorough training. After volunteering each one of us was investigated by the FBI to assess if we were suitable. They looked into our background,

Naturally when "all American girls" arrived on the scene they received a special welcome from GIs. Members of the first contingent of American Red Cross nurses to arrive in England to staff military hospitals, out on their first London pass, meet GIs at the Milestone Club, Kensington.

including our education. There was a good deal of prejudice against women in the services in some quarters, the authorities wanted to be sure that the first girls they got would be the best. We had the same pay as men of equivalent rank and the Army intended that we be treated as equals. We maintained our battalion was the cream of the crop and I don't think the same high standard was expected of later WAC battalions."

WACs were good ambassadors for American womanhood and highly thought of by the British with whom they made friends. One GI ladies' man observed that "we would never have got away behaving with a WAC as we did with the English girls. I don't know a guy who even tried". While another felt "I was a little uneasy in the company of a WAC. It was like being with a sister who might tell Mom".

One in seven US servicemen were already married before coming overseas. A few "played around" and cases of bigamy are recorded. But conduct was predominantly that of faithfulness. Even more men had sweethearts back home and a still greater number didn't date the girls who became their wives until after the war. Some of these girls were later to get an inkling of the good times their spouses had enjoyed in bachelor days in England. Kay Fielding recounts her suspicions with humour:

"Buzz and I were married in 1945 after he

The first company of WACs to arrive in the UK marching into the Reception Centre at Stone on 19 July 1943.

got back from England. We were both from the same small town, but hadn't dated until he came home from overseas. I'd written to several service men during the war and was familiar with V mail and sometimes mail had been censored and blacked out. So when Buzz showed me his diary he'd kept during months in England and I saw some of the things inked out I thought they were military secrets..... For years I thought that until one day it dawned on me they weren't military secrets, but his secrets..... After all those years to his dismay he couldn't remember what he'd blacked out ... or so he said!

In 1972 we made a trip to England; my and Buzz's first since 1944. On a bus tour to Cambridge the tour guide told us we'd stop at 'Dorothy's Tea Room' for lunch. Buzz said that was where he use to hang out when he was on liberty. My response was, "You can tell your Mother you hung out in a tea room, but I'm not that gullible." Well, when we went up the stairs and I saw the bar and the ballroom in the back, I had to eat my words."

Only a few American wives had an opportunity to join their husbands in the UK, Hollywood actress Ellen Drew being one. Her husband, Major Sy Bartlett, was a long-time member of 8th Air Force public relations who, after the war, co-operated with another 8th Air Force veteran, Beirne Lay, in writing *Twelve O' Clock High*, which starred Gregory Peck.

Like most young Americans of my time I went looking for adventure and was certainly not afraid of strange places or customs. Naturally the main focus for adventures was the opposite sex. On my first evening pass after arriving at Raydon Wood I went to Colchester. There I got into conversation with a girl I met in the main street and we got along famously. She was married to a British soldier who was serving overseas but this didn't appear to inhibit her. On the next date she brought along her sister who appeared most anxious to meet a Yank. Here I was with two girls and one was all I could handle. So I had to do some fast thinking. We were outside the Red Cross Club in Colchester and just then I happened to see a GI come out the door. I told the girls to wait where they were while I walked over to this guy and said, "Are you interested in a real nice date?" My luck was in: "Hell, yes!" he said. So I took him over and introduced him to the girls; "This is a good buddy of mine." The truth was I'd never before seen him in my life. Could hardly see him anyway because of the blackout – couldn't see the sister for that matter. Anyhow, these two paired up and solved my problem.

A very nice friendship developed with the Colchester girl but our stay at Raydon was short and the group moved to another base around 25 miles north-east. Around this time I was sent up to a base near Grimsby on detached service. To get there I had to first catch a train to London. Being a city boy I took the opportunity to look around and decided this was the place for me. So from then on whenever I got my monthly three-day pass I was off to London. Found a nice little pub in Kensington High Street. The blonde at the back of the bar took my fancy and I thought maybe I can do something here. I started by buying her drinks and it was soon obvious the interest was mutual. She was another married girl and her husband was a Jap prisoner, having been picked up at Singapore. We dated regularly and she brightened life considerably for this 22 year-old. Thousands of miles from home and without the inhibiting influence of family and the local community, there was no check on the randy tendencies of a young man at that time of life. In my trips to London I got to know the underground system very well. Sometimes I'd see Britishers standing around on a platform looking lost. I'd go up and offer to give directions. Got a kick out of the look on their faces when a Yank told them which train to catch.

I could usually only get to London once a month and there were attractions nearer to hand. When Jerry started launching buzz-bombs from out over the North Sea, the British moved in AA guns around our base, which was close to the coast. Several of these batteries were partly crewed by ATS girls. For we GIs it was like shooting fish in a barrel, there were so many of these girls at the social events. We also discovered the Palais de Dance at Lowestoft, a small port with a heavy Royal Navy presence. Fourteen of us went there to give a buddy who had volunteered for the infantry a good send-off. Whether it was the

glasses of gin and orange or the GIs that attracted them I don't know, but we soon found we had a host of the navy girls, Wrens, round our table. However, my local attraction was an air force girl, a WAAF who was based at the radar directional station near Dunwich. She was single, a nice girl and good fun. Yes, I enjoyed my adventures in England.
Art Swanson

In 1944 I was ferrying aircraft out of Warton after completing 33 missions with the 93rd Bomb Group at Hardwick. After delivering a plane to a base on the south coast and finding no quarters available, two officers and I went into Brighton looking for a hotel. As we walked out of the train station a taxi pulled up and the girl passenger asked if we were looking for a place to stay. She explained that she had a large home and, as her contribution to the war effort, she offered free quarters to military people since the hotels in town were usually full.

We were quite sceptical but, since she was a conservatively dressed, average looking girl in her late twenties, we figured we had little to lose. The taxi took us to a large, gloomy house and we were ushered into a drawing room with one wall of tennis trophies. The girl introduced herself as Doris Dillon and mentioned that she had been a ranking tennis player before the war.

After giving each of us a room, she offered to call two girl friends so that we could all go out to dinner. We agreed, the girls arrived and we went to dinner with Doris as my date. Doris was pretty far out and seemed to have all sorts of hang ups. She complained of a tooth ache and explained that she couldn't go to a dentist because of what happened to her mother. It seems that her mother had a great fear of dentists but was finally forced to visit one because of severe dental problems. She died of fright in the dentist's chair! It was an entertaining evening simply because Doris was so unusual.

We flew back to Warton the next day and, about a week later, a note arrived from Doris saying that she might come up to visit me. After I replied that I was constantly delivering planes around Europe and was never sure of my time at Warton, she phoned and said that she was coming up next weekend anyway. Just before the weekend, as I was frantically trying to get an over the weekend flight, a note arrived from Doris saying, "I can't make it this weekend since I am getting married but how about next weekend?" I wrote back and said that I was too virtuous to go out with married women.
Tom Parry

I started to go to dances when I was 16 years old and one Saturday night I went with some friends to the Oddfellows Hall at Weldon. The music was Glenn Miller, who was playing live over the radio. There were large windows in the hall with big sills on which we girls put our handbags. While I was dancing a group of Americans came in and sat on the chairs below the window where we girls had been sitting. When I went to get my handbag I said, "Excuse me, can I get my bag." And this Yank says, "I'll think about it." Cheeky so-and-so. Anyway, he asked me to dance to *In The Mood* and later he wanted to take me home. Now we girls had heard lots of things about these Yanks and were not sure what we might be getting ourselves into. So if you let one you weren't sure about take you home then the thing was to take him to the wrong house so he didn't know where you lived. My mother had no time for Americans but a few nights later she came in and said, "There'a a Yank walking up and down the road outside with a torch and asking for you." As she was worried what the neighbours would think she told me to go out and ask him to come in. It was the same fellow and it was the start of our courtship.

One night I lent him my brand new bicycle to go back to his base. The next I heard he'd got burned in an explosion and was detained in Lilford hospital. While he was there I borrowed a bike and cycled the 30 miles round trip to see him. When he came out he found my new bike had been stolen, but he promised that one day he'd buy me another one. We married in the summer of 1944 when I was 17 and went to London for our honeymoon. The flying bombs were coming over at that time and we heard one's engine stop, which meant it was about to drop and explode, at just the wrong moment, for it wasn't the only thing that got out of control. Our son was born the following year and we always said he was conceived with a bang. It took Bob a long while to keep his promise, but eventually, after eight grandchildren, he did buy me a new bike.
Stella Auger

Film star Marlene Dietrich links arms with Colonel William Seawell and Captain Lawrence Pfeiffer on arriving to entertain the men at Deenethorpe on 29 September 1944. She wears an ETO service ribband on her USO uniform. Marlene was flown from an airfield near Birmingham in a Fortress called *Pakawulp*. The next day the bomber was shot down over Germany. The superstitious made a mental note not to fly celebrities in combat aircraft.

HOWEVER anti-American an individual may have been, all reasoned Britishers knew in their heart of hearts that victory would have been exceptionally difficult, if not impossible, without the United States' massive industrial capacity and vast manpower. In any case, initial suspicion and prejudice towards GIs rapidly disappeared among those who got to know them, or came to terms with their presence. The impact of two or three thousand young men from a foreign land suddenly set down in a rural East Anglian environment was considerable; for many villages it was the most extraordinary happening in their history. Parishioners with an airfield spread across their acres best appreciated the USAAF's part in the air war. Many such people did count the warplanes out and count them back and talked of "our boys" with as much fervour or sorrow as if these young Americans were kinsmen. They came to appreciate the genuine kindness of the average American and to admire his resourcefulness. Conversely, the US airman came to understand that British "reserve" was no bar to friendship and to admire the fortitude of this nation.

A common theme of praise was the generally cool nature of the British under aerial bombardment. One young officer relates:

"On my first visit to London the air raid warning sounded and I ran towards the nearest shelter, only to realise that everyone else in the street appeared to ignore the wailing noise. Somewhat shamefacedly I was about to continue my walk when the unmistakable sound of a V-1 approaching again made me run for the shelter. At its entrance I turned to see people hesitating and looking skywards, but as soon as the missile had passed over, they continued on their way as if nothing had happened. On future visits I learned to take it like the natives and live with the buzz-bombs".

With so many young Americans in their midst it was inevitable that some US "culture" should rub off on the locals. In addition to slang and terminology, many younger generation Britons became addicted to the music of the "big bands" – Benny Goodman, Artie Shaw, Harry James and particularly Glenn Miller - and to indulge their fancy tuned in to the American Forces Network that never failed to broadcast this kind of music following its UK airwaves debut on Independence Day 1943. Enthusiasm for these bands in Britain certainly equalled that in the USA as did the popularity of several American vocalists of whom Bing Crosby undoubtedly was "the tops". America was also absorbed from the copies of *Stars and Stripes* daily newspaper and *Yank* magazine which, although produced in the UK by and for the US forces, had a good sized readership in British homes.

There was even some addiction to US sports. Walter Bergstrom remembers:

"Of the ten men in our basketball team, nine were combat fliers. We'd go round to the different air bases and I was always surprised to see so many British people in the crowd. They would root and cheer for us kids. It was real nice. We got to the finals for the 8th Air Force Championship but got beaten by a bunch of medics."

Reciprocal interest in sport was meagre. Few Americans took to cricket, which most considered a bore, and soccer was only occasionally indulged. Golf, on the other hand, was practised by those who already had the habit and at least one Norfolk airfield had an improvised course. USAAF personnel were eager supporters of athletics meetings and also organised international events. The British were also familiar with the image of the cowboy, which to most – again through Hollywood - was the most prominent American character of all. In the winter of 1943 a rodeo was staged at Carrow Road football ground in Norwich, up to that time the biggest piece of entertainment set up by the Americans in the UK. Over 7,000 spectators were drawn to watch "bronco busting", steer riding, rope twirling and other activities associated with the Wild

Above: Many stations had their own bands. The ten-piece Flying Eagles served Debden, Essex.

The legendary Glenn Miller posed for this photograph at the request of Captain John Woolnough during the AAF Band's visit to Attlebridge on 18 August 1944. The venue amused Miller, who commented that he had never before had his picture taken in a urinal.

West. The proceeds, some £700, went towards charities.

American participation in fund-raising activities was always prominent, particularly in connection with children. The interchange of goodwill that existed is well illustrated in the following account from Major Newton McLaughlin, an administrative officer at 2nd Air Division:

"We arrived in Norfolk close to Christmas 1942 and our first friends in the area were farmers. One cut down a huge pine tree for us to use for Christmas in the Bishops Palace and several farmers invited our men

Above left: Comedian Bob Hope, with Frances Langford, wisecracking to the 303rd Bomb Group at Molesworth, July 1943. Hope was one of the most popular entertainers with US servicemen.

Above right: Cameras click as Vivien Leigh addresses the crowd assembled on the occasion of the christening of Fortress *Stage Door Canteen* by Winston Churchill's daughter, Mary, at Ridgewell, Essex in April 1944.

The two most famous Hollywood celebrities serving in England were Clark Gable and James Stewart. Gable, a Captain, arrived in April 1943 to make a gunnery film, flying five combat missions before returning to the USA later that year. James Stewart arrived in November 1943 as CO of a Liberator Squadron. Initially based at Tibenham, he was later deputy CO at Old Buckenham before taking a staff appointment at Ketteringham Hall, where he remained until after VE-Day. Also at Old Buckenham, but then a sergeant serving on ground duties, was Walter Matheau, who was to achieve Hollywood fame in post-war years.

Boys being taught the mysteries of baseball, "a sort of rounders" to them. Worth setting up a pose to record another aspect of Anglo-American goodwill.

to their homes for dinner. Their warmth and kindness can never be forgotten. Lady Teichman kindly offered to let us use her tennis courts, which we speedily put to good use. We had heard of English Christmas carols so we organised a group of carollers to go into the villages near our base to sing; but the villagers didn't seem familiar with the custom and didn't quite understand what we were doing. Our servicemen invited the evacuated children to their bases as guests for Christmas dinner. They also took them to the theatre in Norwich to see 'Goodie Two-Shoes' in pantomime. Our boys also called on British service hospitals and passed out cigarettes and cheered the men whenever possible. The people of Norwich furnished our men with golf balls and permitted them to use the golf courses.

A Norwich author and historian donated many hours of his time taking our men on historic tours and lecturing on local English history. One day, when our hill-billy band was entertaining wounded Canadians billeted in Norfolk, an elderly English gentleman who was an authority on folk songs advised us that the songs being sung were ancient English in origin. One day some enlisted men asked permission to share their rations with the Jenny Lind Crippled Children's Hospital. After an inspection by our surgeon and chaplain our Co agreed.

We then adopted this hospital and at Christmas time called with a truckload of presents and a hill-billy band. On leaving, a gentleman was waiting outside to thank us and invited us to his home for tea. He said he was a publisher of a newspaper and thought he could help us, which he did. His name was Tom Copeman and I cannot say enough for the splendid assistance he gave us in every direction. He did more than anyone to cement relationships between the Yanks and the English."

While the girls and the pubs were the main attractions, sight-seeing was also an earnestly pursued pastime. Sight-seeing revealed history and few GIs had hitherto known that it was from the locality that they occupied in force, that many notable founders of the American nation had originated. The Pilgrim Fathers, several of whom were from eastern counties of England, had sailed in a Harwich ship with a Harwich captain and the vessel was probably built at that port or Ipswich. Eighteen years before, in 1602, a native of Grundisburgh, Suffolk, Bartholomew Gosnold, had reached the North American coast, and discovered and named Cape Cod. In 1606 the squire of Otley set out from Ipswich in the *Godspeed* and, with two other vessels, reached and settled in

Rowing his girl on the Cam. (Mark Brown/Air Force Academy)

VE-Day night celebrations at Eye airfield. Pyrotechnics used for signalling were a good substitute for fireworks.(Arnold Delmonico)

Virginia. Of ships following the *Mayflower* in the seventeenth century, several left from East Anglian ports carrying such notables as John Winthrop of Groton, who founded Boston and was the first Governor of Massachusetts, John Samuel Lincoln of Hingham, Norfolk, the great-great-great-great-grandfather of Abraham and John Washington whose father was vicar at Purleigh, Essex, the great-grand-father of George. Connections between this old world and the new were numerous.

By VE-Day, 8th May 1945, only a few 9th Air Force units and those under the First Allied Airborne Army remained in the UK. The service and supply organisations under the United States Strategic Air Forces in Europe were still prominent in the Midlands and north-west England but the main USAAF strength remained with the 8th Air Force in East Anglia. With peace, departure from the UK was rapid. Some units were gone in a few weeks and the heavy bomber groups began flying their Fortresses and Liberators home across the Atlantic in mid-May, a movement completed in six weeks. Each aircraft carried its ground crew and the remaining ground personnel often sailed as they had arrived, on one or other of the Queens. By July the only bomber groups remaining were those selected to remain on occupational duties in Europe and these, too, soon transferred to the Continent. The fighter group personnel were the last to sail, their aircraft having been broken up for salvage or stored. Few airfield bases had occupants by November and Honington, the last, was officially closed in February 1946.

For individual GIs eager to go home the immediate preoccupation was one of "points". This was a system based on length of service and other factors which required 85 points for immediate shipment home and discharge, which only applied to a minority serving in the UK. Thousands of GI brides had to wait until the servicemen had been transported, although some had sailed prior to the end of hostilities when there was space in east-west crossings.

The GI brides' entry to the USA was not easy; marriage to an American citizen did not automatically transfer that citizenship to the wife. Every girl had to fill in copious forms and provide various documents, not only for validity, but to ensure that she would be supported once she arrived in the USA. To most these requirements seemed obstructional, as if the US authority resented this influx of foreign women. The official requirements, if overdone in some respects, proved valid for there were to be sad cases of girls who changed their minds and refused to leave the UK, and others where wives found, on arrival, that they had been deserted. These were only a very small percentage of the total, as were those marriages that faltered in the early post-war years. The divorce rate among Anglo-American couples is said to have been far below that of any other contemporary group in the USA.

Perhaps the most extraordinary aspect of this Second World War friendly invasion has been the continuing bond of goodwill between those "here" with those "over there", from whichever side of the Atlantic it is viewed. Across the years a succession of veterans have returned to their wartime haunts, probably because airmen cannot revisit a battlefield in the sky and the old airfield sites become the focal points of interest. On the British side it is seeing these men and women keeping faith with their past that has touched

In 1945 the personnel of the 2nd Air Division – the men who flew the Liberators in 8th Air Force – put their hands in their pockets and donated to a memorial for those of the organisation who had lost their lives. The fund was used to build and stock an American Memorial Library Room in Norwich Central Library.

emotions and brought a sincere welcome. Most individual veterans' groups have links with supporters in the vicinity of their old bases, who tend memorials and promote welcomes back. As a speculation, no body of foreign military veterans, has had such an enduring rapport with the local indigenous population of the country in which they served. But then the nature of the offensive air war as pursued from England and the situation of the combatants oscillating between heaven and hell was indeed unique.

GI brides line the decks as the SS *Argentina* prepares to sail from Southampton. (Imperial War Museum)

May 1945 and a group of British well-wishers at Horsham St Faith, Norfolk, wave off a Liberator at the start of its journey back to the USA.

In a moment of danger the British always seemed to come up with a laugh. I was sitting in a London movie theater watching Ginger Rogers in 'Lady In The Dark'. The hero had just taken the heroine in his arms and we knew the inevitable kiss was not far away. At that moment the unmistakable engine noise of a V-1 flying bomb could clearly be heard and then ceased abruptly, meaning it was on its way down. Immediately a voice from the balcony yelled out: 'For God's sake KISS HER before it's too late!' I don't know if it was the laughter or the explosion of the bomb that shook the building but plenty of dust was stirred up.

John Lusk Moore

British	American
accumulator	chargeable battery
adjustable spanner	monkey wrench
autumn	fall
bags (trousers)	slacks
bank holiday	legal day
banknote	bill
barrow	push cart
bed	cot
bill	cheque
billiards saloon	poolroom
biscuit	cookie
biscuit	sectional mattress
bitter	ale
blind	window shade
bloke	guy
bobby	cop
bonnet (car)	hood
booking office	ticket office
boot	shoe (high)
boot (car)	trunk
bootlace/shoelace	shoestring
bowler hat	derby
braces	suspenders
caretaker	janitor
cigarette end	butt
charabanc	rubberneck wagon
chemist shop	drugstore
chips	french fried potatoes
cinema	movie house
cockerel	rooster
collar stud	collar button
combinations	union suit or long johns
conscription	draft
contraceptives	rubbers
cream cracker	soda biscuit
crisps	potato chips
cupboards	closet
curtains	drapes
dickey (car)	rumble seat
draughts	checkers
drawing pin	thumb tack
dressing gown	bath robe
dungarees	overalls
dustbin	ash can
dynamo	generator
earth wire	ground wire
elevator	farm conveyor
face flannel	washrag
fanlight	transon
fillet (beef)	tenderloin
first floor	second floor
fishmonger	fish seller
flat	apartment
flicks	movies
foyer	lobby
french beans	string beans
fruiterer	fruit seller
full stop	period
galoshes	rubber boots
gangway	aisle
garden	yard
gear lever	gear shift
geyser	water heater
geyser (slang)	a man
goods waggon	freight car
gramophone	phonograph
greatcoat	trenchcoat
grilled	broiled
guard (rail)	conductor
gum	mucilage
handbag	purse
hawker	huckster
hire purchase	instalment purchase
hoarding	billboard
homely	ugly
hood (car)	soft top
ill	sick
interval	intermission
ironmongery	hardware
joint (meat)	roast
jug	pitcher
kiosk	booth
kipper	smoked herring
ladder (hose)	run
lager	beer
leave	on pass
level crossing	grade crossing (rail)
lift	elevator
lodger	roomer
lorry	truck
lounge suit	business suit
luggage	baggage
mac (mackintosh)	raincoat
marrow (vegetable)	squash
meths (methylated spirits)	denatured alcohol
mineral water	soft drink
motorcar	automobile (auto)
music hall	vaudeville
nappy	diaper
nursing home	rest hospital
overalls	fatigues
pack (cards)	deck
pants (mens)	drawers
paraffin	coal oil or low cost fuel
parcel	package
parking lot	car park
pavement	sidewalk

petrol	gasolene or gas	variety	vaudeville
pillar box	mail box	verge (road)	shoulder
post (a letter)	mail	vest	undershirt
postponed or			
deferred	rainchecked	waistcoat	vest
pram	baby carriage	walking stick	cane
pub	drinking saloon	wardrobe	closet
pullover	sweater	washbasin	washbowl
		whisky and soda	highball
queue	stand in line	windscreen (car)	windshield
		wing or mudguard	
race course	race track	(car)	fender
railway	railroad	wire	telegram
railway carriage	passenger car	wireless	radio
righto	okay		
ring (telephone)	call		
rubber	eraser		
rubbish	junk or garbage		
saloon (car)	sedan		
scent spray	atomiser		
scenic railway	roller coaster		
scone	biscuit		
seaside	beach		
shingle	pebbly beach		
shop	store		
shooting	hunting		
shopwalker	floorwalker		
showey woman	broad		
sick	vomit		
silencer (car)	muffler		
sitting room	living room		
skittle alley	bowling alley		
sledge	sled		
sofa	davenport		
solicitor	lawyer		
sparking plug	spark plug		
spirits	hard liquor		
spirit lamp	alcohol lamp		
staircase	stairway		
stalls	orchestra seats		
sticking plaster	adhesive tape		
stroller	pushchair		
sump (car)	oil pan		
suspenders	garters (socks)		
sweets (meal)	dessert		
sweets	candies		
swissroll	jellyroll		
tap	spigot		
tart	pie		
taxi	cab		
ten pin bowling	nine pin bowling		
tin opener	can opener		
tip	garbage dump		
toffee	taffy		
top of the bill	topliner		
torch	flashlight		
town centre	downtown		
tram	trolley		
treacle	syrup		
truncheon	nightstick		
trunk call	long distance call		
turn ups (trousers)	cuffs		
two-seater (car)	roadster		
underground	subway		
valve (radio)	tube		

Index

A

Abbot, Earl, 67
Acton, Suffolk, 54
Ades, Lou, 14
Aircraft
  A-20 Havoc, 26, 27
  B-17 Fortress, 19, 20, 21, 22, 23, 24, 25, 81
  B-24 Liberator, 18, 21, 22, 23, 25, 79, 81, 82, 83
  B-25 Mitchell, 22
  B-26 Marauder, 22, 23, 24, 25, 26, 28, 51
  Boston, 7
  C-47 Skytrain, 21, 27, 28
  Curtiss flying boat, 4
  P-38 Lightning, 24, 25, 26
  P-47 Thunderbolt, 18, 25, 26, 27
  P-51 Mustang, 18, 26, 29
  Spitfire, 25
American Red Cross, 31, 32, 33, 35, 36, 46, 54, 73, 74, 75
Anderson, Sgt., 37
SS *Andes*, 7
Anglo-American Clubs, 33
SS *Argentina*, 82
Armstrong, Roger, 41, 46
Arnold, Gen. H.H., 6
Astaire, Adèle, 32
Astaire, Fred, 32
Aston, Staffs, 34
Atcham, Shropshire, 7
Attlebridge, Norfolk, 39, 51, 78
Auger, Stella, 76

B

Bamber Bridge, Lancs, 58
Bamman, Henry, 39
Barnett, William, 71
Bartlett, Sy, 75
Bassingbourn, 14, 22, 41, 45, 46, 68, 72
Bawdeswell, Norfolk, 39
Bedford, 48, 67
Bedser, Mrs, 52
Belfast, 5, 51
Bergstrom, Walter, 78
Birmingham, 77
Bodney, 67
Bolton, Elco, 58
Boston, 7
Boxted, 37, 62
Bradford, 63, 64
Brigstock, 42
Broughton, Northants, 60
Brown, Ivan, 16, 47
Bryant, John, 12, 42
Bull Hotel, Cambridge, 32
Bungay, 68
Bures, 24
Burtonwood, 7
Bury St Edmunds, 8, 23, 41, 45, 66
Bushey Hall, Watford, 14, 73
Bushy Park, Teddington, 6, 36

C

Cambridge, 32, 44, 48, 68, 74, 81
Carpole, F., 37
Castle Acre, 47
Catworth, Hunts, 43
Cavendish, Lady, 32
Cayer, Robert, 72
Chamberlain, Bud, 68

Chaney, Maj. Gen. J.E., 6
Charles St, London, 32
Chatham, 66
Chauncey, Brig. Gen. C.C., 36
Cheddington, 44
Chelveston, 22, 40
Cheltenham, 15
Chipping Ongar, 28, 63
Church Army, 34
Churchill, Winston, 10
Churchill, Mary, 79
Chute, Daphne, 15, 49
Clark, Forrest, 44
Clyde, 15, 55
Coffin, Robert, 42
Colchester, 9, 44, 47, 57, 62, 66, 75
Collar, George, 34, 53
Collins, H.W., 18
Connington, Hunts, 8
Cooper, Edgar, 57
Cooper, Tom, 10
Copeman, Tom, 80
Covent Garden, 70
Coyle, Peter, 34
Cranford, Northants, 15
Culford, 70

D

Debach, 56, 59, 63
Debden, 43, 69, 78
Dedham, 57
Deenethorpe, 37, 72, 77
DeLuce, Florence, 67
Denham, Suffolk, 53
Dereham, East, 54
Diddington, 47
Dietrich, Marlene, 77
Diss, 9, 48
Dog, Brampton, 47
Dog, Grundisburgh, 59
Doherty, William, 44
Doolittle, James H., 45
Drew, Ellen, 75
Dunstable, 44
Dunwich, 76

E

Eagle, Cambridge, 43
Eaker, Gen. Ira, 5, 35, 58
Eastleigh, 4
East Wretham, 71
Eisenhower, Gen., 58
Eye, Suffolk, 81
Eynsham Hall, Oxon, 39

F

Falcone, Iris, 69
Fellows, Ward, 15
Fen Ditton, 46
Fielding, Kay, 74
Framlingham, 36, 37, 38
Fredericks, Elenor, 10, 42
Frost, Willie, 42
Fox, Catworth, 43

G

Gable, Clark, 79
Giacomini, Alfred, 7
Godspeed, 80

Glasgow, 40, 55
Goldsmith, Capt., 54
Goodman, Benny, 78
Goodson, James, 69
Gosnold, Bartholomew, 80
Grafton Underwood, 7, 36, 71
Great Yeldham, 44
Green, Joan, 63, 64
Greenacre, Tom and Ken, 52
Greenham Common, 21
Griffiss, Townsend, 6
Grimsby, 75
Groton, 81
Grosvenor House Hotel, London, 32
Grundisburgh, 59, 80

H
Halesworth, 3, 16, 52, 68
Hardwick, 76
Harkins, Charles, 52
Harrington, 72
Harwich, 80
Hennesay, Edward, 42
Hepburn, Katharine, 2
Hethel, 11, 12, 56
Hethersett, 70
High Wycombe, 7
Hill, Calvin, 49
Hill, Warren, 68
Hingham, 81
Hintlesham, 55
Hitcham, 72
Honingham Hall, Norfolk, 51
Honington, 48, 82
Hope, Bob, 32, 79
Horham, Suffolk, 56
Horsham St Faith, 70, 83
HRH King George VI, 35
HRH Princess Elizabeth, 45
Howland, John, 38, 49
Hunter, Brig. Gen., 14
Huntingdon, 35, 47, 48
Huntingfield, Lady Joan, 67
Hutchinson, Walter, 53
Hyde Park, London, 56

I
Ibsley, 8
Ipswich, 50, 58, 72, 80

J
James, Harry, 78
Johnson, R., 10
Jenny Lind Hospital, Norwich, 80
Jones, Albert, 35, 54

K
Kegelman, Charles, 7
Kelly, Walter, 37
Kensington, 74, 75
Kerns, Margaret, 67
Kerr, Robert, 30
Kettering, 9, 60
Ketteringham Hall, Norfolk, 79
Killingholme, 4
Kimbolton, 66
Kings Cliffe, 15
Klette, Immanuel, 67
Knettishall, 71
Kupferman, Saul, 33

L
Laidlaw, William, 59
Langar, 6
Langford, Frances, 79
Lanford Lodge, 7
Lashenden, 18

Laube, Edward, 32
Lavenham, 11, 43, 56
Lay, Beirne, 75
Leber, Col. Harry, 79
Lee, Ira, 54
Leeds, 63, 64
Leigh, Vivien, 79
Lessig, Cecil, 6
Lewis, Adeline and Lloyd, 39
Lilford, 76
Lincoln, Samuel, 81
Link, C. M., 16
Little Bromley, 57
Liverpool, 5
Loch Lomond, 10
London, 10, 16, 32, 47, 49, 56, 57, 66, 69, 75, 83
Londonderry, 5
Longfellow, Brig. Gen. Newton, 35
Lord Haw-Haw, 62
Lowestoft, 75
Lunt, Alfred, 79

M
Madingley, 25
Mahurin, Walker, 73
Marcus, James, 37
Marlborough Head, Dedham, 57
Maravell, Helen, 52, 73
Marshall, Jean, 70
Marshall, Gen. George, 6
Mason, Joe, 67
Mason, Lloyd, 35
Matthews, Nelson, 57
Mayflower, 80
McLaughlin, Newton, 78
Middleton, Suffolk, 55
Military units
    1 BW, 10, 22, 35
    2 Wing, 22
    2 Air Div., 70, 78, 82
    3 Air Div., 28, 36, 54
    3 Wing, 22, 23
    4 SAD, 72
    4 Wing, 22
    5 Wing, 22
    8 AF, 22, 23, 26, 27, 28, 29, 30, 35, 67, 81
    VIII FC, 14
    VIII BC, 35
    9 AF, 26, 27, 30, 81
    12 AF, 22
    15 AF, 26
    15 B Sqd., 7
    34 Inf. Div., 5
    44 BG, 47
    55 Arm. Div., 62
    56 FG, 73
    64 Sqd. RAF, 6
    66 FW, 70
    91 BG, 41
    93 BG, 76
    94 BG, 45
    94 F. Sqd., 8
    97 BG, 59
    100 BG, 9, 48
    226 Sqd. RAF, 7
    303 BG, 11, 42, 79
    306 BG, 33
    325 SG, 40
    351 BG, 10, 57
    354 FG, 62
    357 FG, 55
    364 FG, 49
    381 BG, 49
    384 BG, 36, 71
    386 BG, 32
    387 BG, 51
    389 BG, 47

390 BG, 36
392 BG, 47
423 B Sqd, 67
445 BG, 34
479 FG, 42
486 BG, 45
493 BG, 32, 69
689 Qm Co, 9
1514 Qm Co, 60
Miller, Glenn, 76, 78
Molesworth, 7, 22, 79
Morrow, Thomas, 10, 60
Moore, John Lusk, 83
Moy, 48
Murphy, Charles, 16
Moose, Philip, 13

N
Nairn, R.E., 53
Neasham, Jack, 15, 40
Newport, 7
Newton Bromswold, 50
Nicoll, Don and Cynthia, 33
Norden, N.L., 19
Norris, Ken, 33
Northampton, 59
Norwich, 9, 35, 56, 78, 80, 82

O
Old Buckenham, 79
Olivier, Laurence, 79
Otley, 80
Oundle, 59

P
Parry, Tom, 76
Partridge, Gen. Earle, 36
Peterborough, 57, 69
Pfeiffer, Lawrence, 77
Piccadilly Commando, 66
Pierce, Col., 39
Polebrook, 59
Post Exchange, 46, 61, 66
Prestwick, 44, 49
Purleigh, 81

Q
Queen Elizabeth, 7
Queen's Hotel Bradford, 64
Quidenham, 39

R
Rackheath, 65
Rainbow Corner, London, 32, 33
Ramsey, John, 39, 64
Raydon, 75
Red, Preston, 11
Redman, Doris and Paul, 38
Regent Street, London, 10
Renshaw, Mary, 55
Richardson, Wilbur, 57
Ridgewell, 44, 62, 79
Ringwood, 8
Robinson, Earl, 42, 62
Robinson, Edward G., 2
Rogers, Ginger, 83
Rogers, Lilburn, 32
Romsey, 53
Roosevelt, F.D., 4, 19
Rouen, 22
Royston, 46, 68
Ruska, Nancy, 70

S
Sajdak, Stanley, 72
Salisbury, 52
Sand, Robert, 13

Sawston, 70
Schilling, David, 3
Searah, Rose, 66
Seawell, William, 77
Seething, 11
Senk, Leon, 61
Shank, M.E., 37
Shaw, Artie, 78
Shapiro, Irving, 45
Shapley, Elizabeth, 67
Sherman, Allen, 51
Shipdham, 34, 44, 54, 68
Sicklesmere, 8
Slater, Charles, 8
Sloan, Alexander, 46
Smart, Curtis, 48
Smith, Marion, 72
Snell, Royal, 11
Snetterton Heath, 13, 36, 37, 39
Southburgh, Norfolk, 47
Southampton, 82
Spaatz, Gen. Carl, 35, 58
Spaldwick, 11
Stage Door Canteen, London, 32
Stanbridge Earls, Hants, 53
Stars and Stripes, 36
Stewart, James, 79
Stone, 34, 38, 74
Stroven, Harvey, 45
Sudbury, 12, 42, 45
Sullivan, Bill, 49
Sutton, James, 67
Swaffham, 47
Swan Lavenham, 43, 56
Swan Newton Bromswold, 50
Swanson, Arthur, 55, 76
Swanton Morley, 7
Sullivan, Bill, 49
Sutton, James, 67

T
Taylor, Charles, 52
Taylor, S., 10
Teddington, 6
Teichman, Sir Eric, 51
Teichman, Lady, 51, 80
Three Cocks, Brigstock, 42
Thetford, 71
Thorpe Abbotts, 36
Thrandeston, Suffolk, 20
Thruxton, 18
Thurleigh, 22, 33, 67
Thurston, 58
Thwaits, Evelyn, 9
Tibenham, 79
Townsend, Lady, 32
Trip, Cecilia, 71
Troston Park, Suffolk, 58
Tyson, James, 38

U
Utal, Jordan, 70

V
Veynar, Hathy, 9

W
Walsh, H. Ben, 56
War Orphans' Fund, 35
Warton, 7, 76
Washington, John, 81
Wattisham, 42
Wedgewood, Josiah, 38
Weldon, 76
Wenger, Mary, 34
Wendling, 47
Wethersfield, 27

Wickstead Park, Northants, 9
White Hart, Yeldham, 44
White, Stanley, 47
Williams, F., 10
Winn, Roy, 72
Winthrop, John, 81
Wivenhoe, 13
Woolnough, John, 78
Wormingford, 17
Wray, Stanley, 45
Wycombe Abbey, 7
Wymondham, 56
Wyton, 4

Y
Yank, 78

Z
Zimmerman, Al, 32, 69

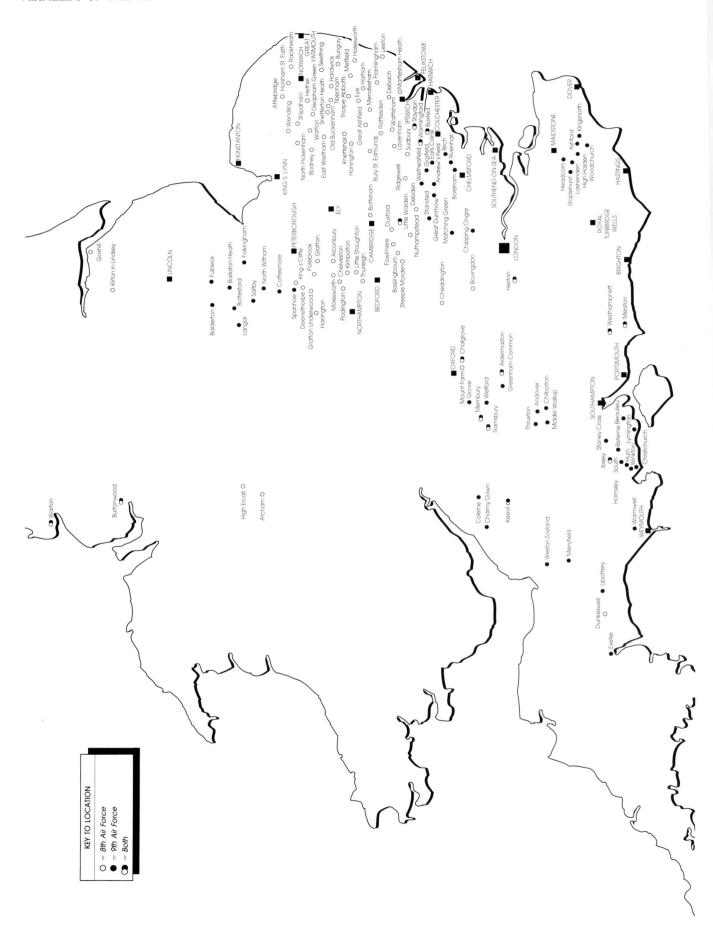

KEY TO LOCATION

○ = 8th Air Force
● = 9th Air Force
◐ = Both